Marko Poloznich

DA
SHIT

Copyright © 2016 by Marko Poloznich

Book design & cover art by Marko Poloznich

All rights reserved. No part of this book may be reproduced by any mechanical, photographic, or electronic process, or any information storage, or retrieval system, transmitted, or otherwise be copied for public or private use-other than for "fair use" without prior written permission of the publisher.

This book is a work of fiction. Names, characters, places and scenes are products of the author's imagination. This book consists of the author's attempt of articulating shit words and does not intend offence to any way of living, race, gender, religeon, group or organization.

The intent of the author is only to help people laugh. In the event you use any of the information in this book for yourself, which is your constitutional right, the author and the publisher assume no responsibility for your actions.

Published in New Zealand by: The Magic
Contact: themagicnz@gmail.com

ISBN 978-0-473-35518-0
ISBN 978-0-473-35657-6 (Kindle)
ISBN 978-0-473-35656-9 (Epub)
ISBN 978-0-473-35658-3 (iBook)

1st printing, April 2016

CONTENTS

Step 1
Understanding this shit 1
Redemption 16

Step 2
Taking it further 17
Dangerous shit 30

Step 3
Recognizing shit 33
Shit cycle 46

Step 4
More shit 49
Shit of the Undead 62

Step 5
Going beyond 65
Positive shit 80

Dedicated to all the
shit word users
worldwide

1

Understanding this shit

It's time to uncover... Da Shit!
Trippy shit
Hey, this shit has absolutely nothing to do with me!
Let's jam this shit!
This guy's a lunatic...

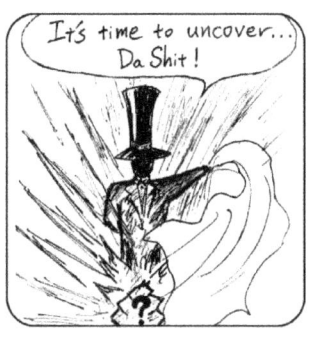

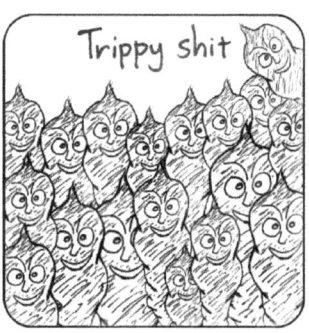

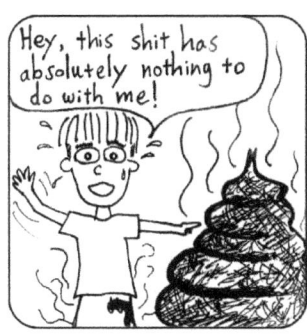

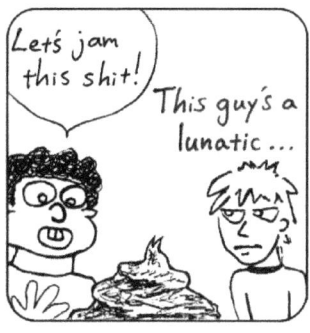

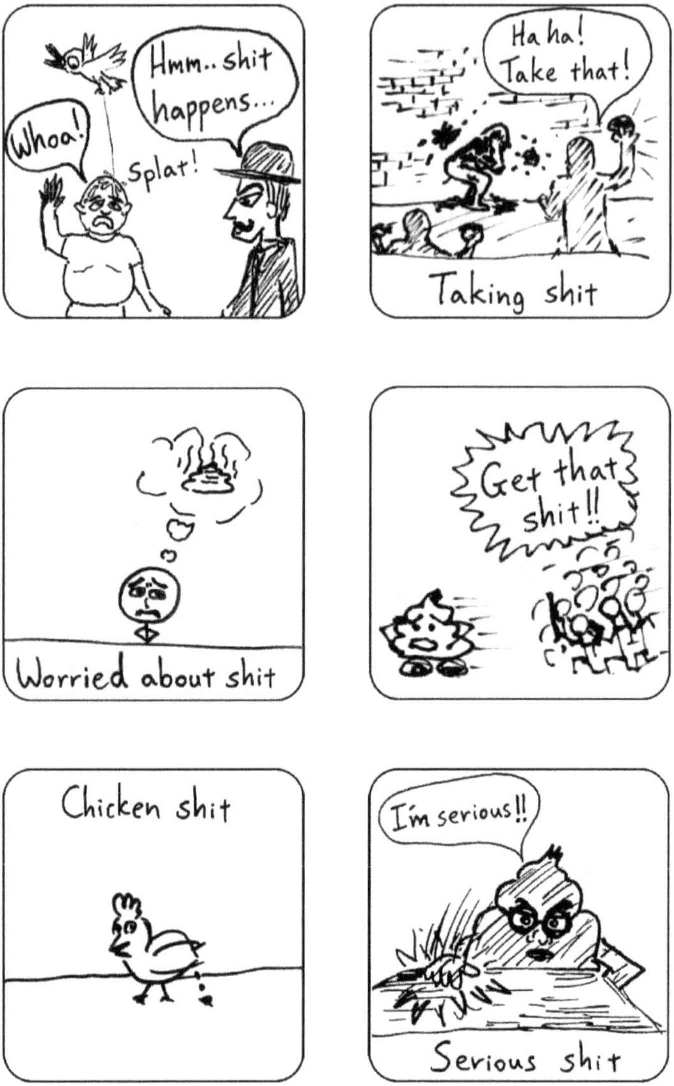
Whoa!
Splat!
Hmm.. shit happens...
Ha ha! Take that!
Taking shit
Worried about shit
Get that shit!!
Chicken shit
I'm serious!!
Serious shit

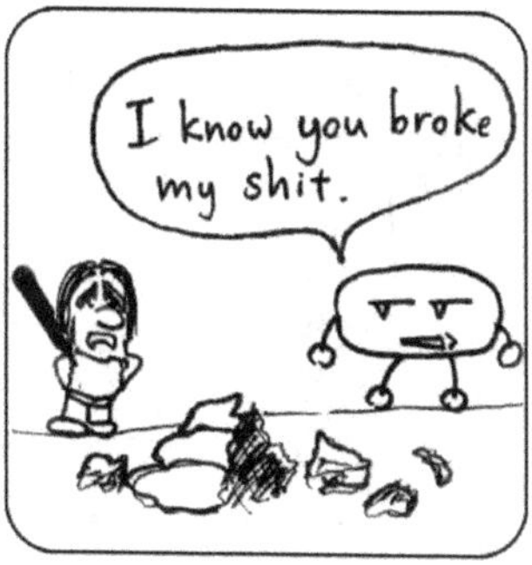
I know you broke my shit.

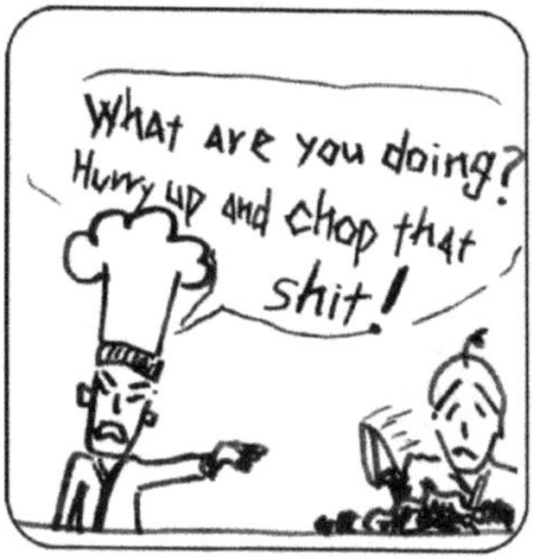
What are you doing? Hurry up and chop that shit!

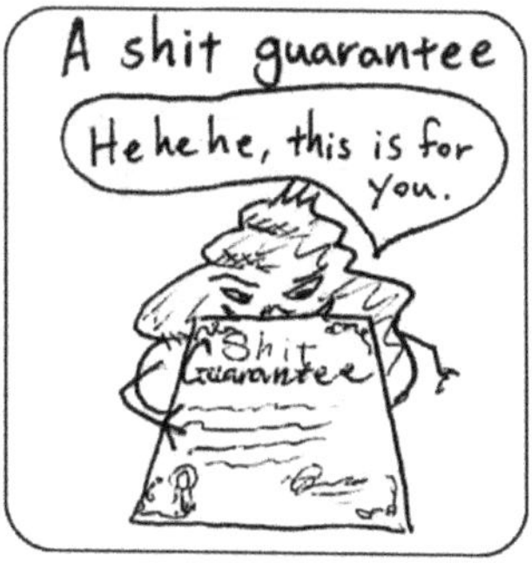
A shit guarantee
Hehehe, this is for you.
Shit guarantee

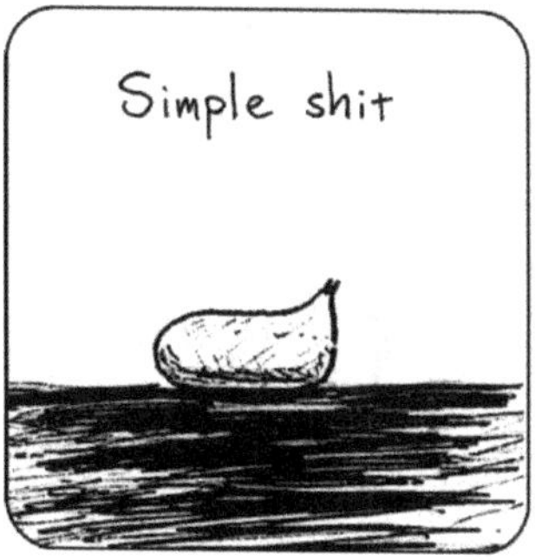
Simple shit

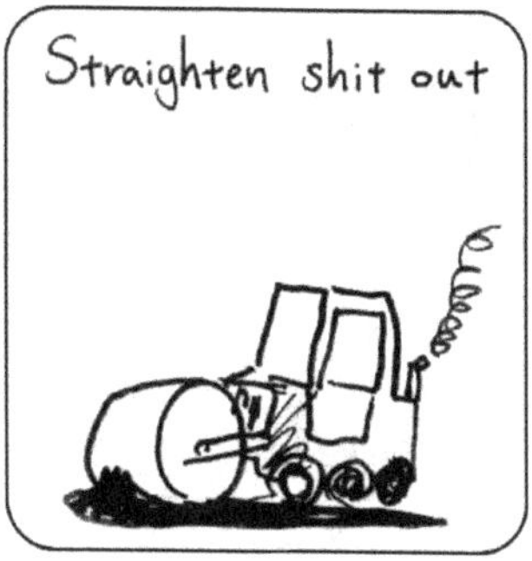
Straighten shit out

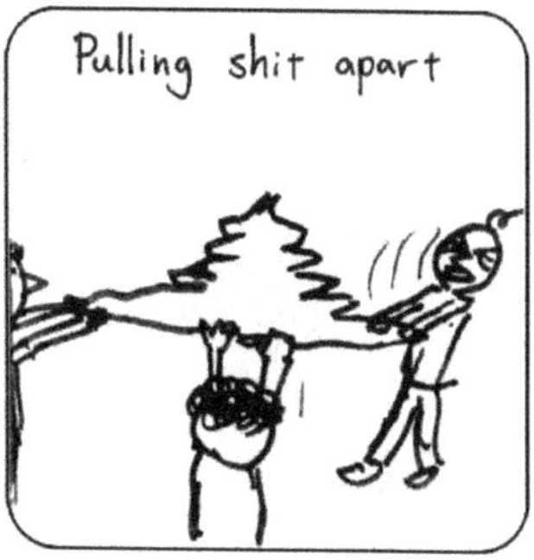
Pulling shit apart

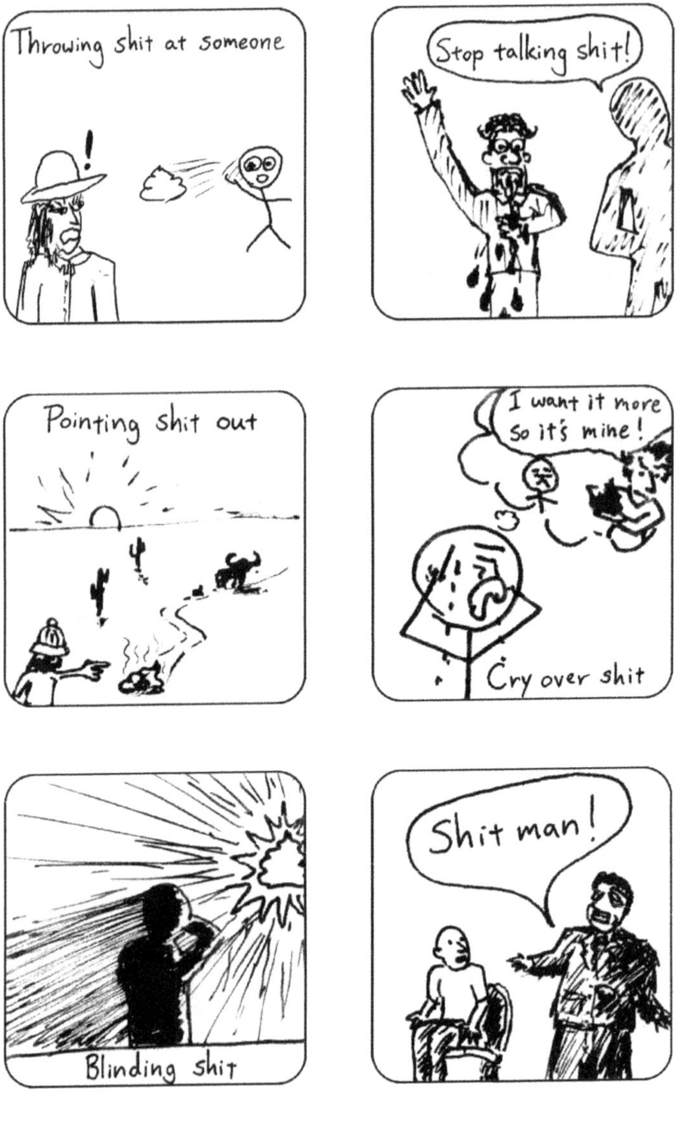
Throwing shit at someone
!
Stop talking shit!
Pointing shit out
I want it more so it's mine!
Cry over shit
Blinding shit
Shit man!

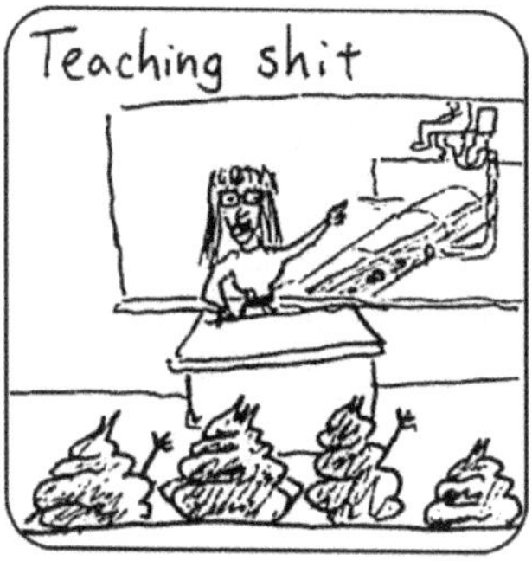
Teaching shit

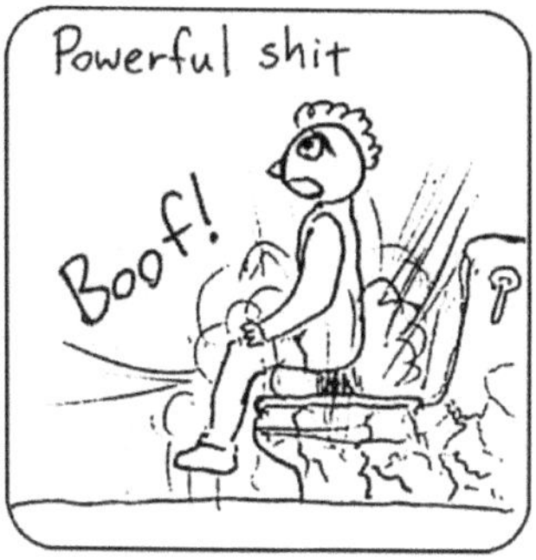
Powerful shit
Boof!

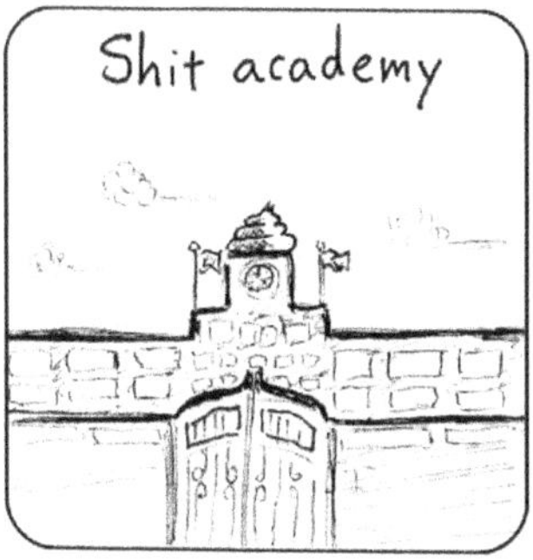
Shit academy

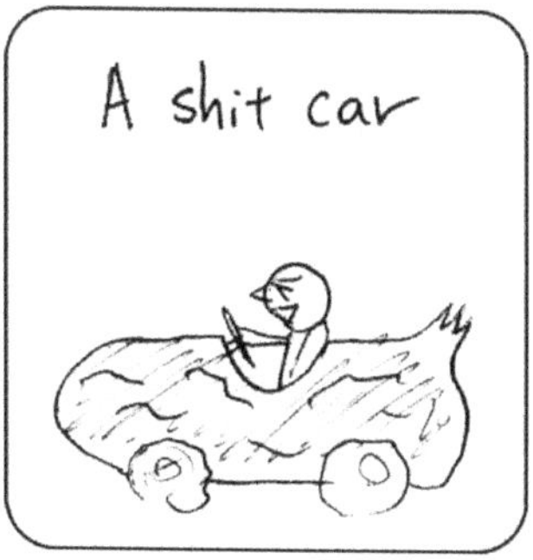
A shit car

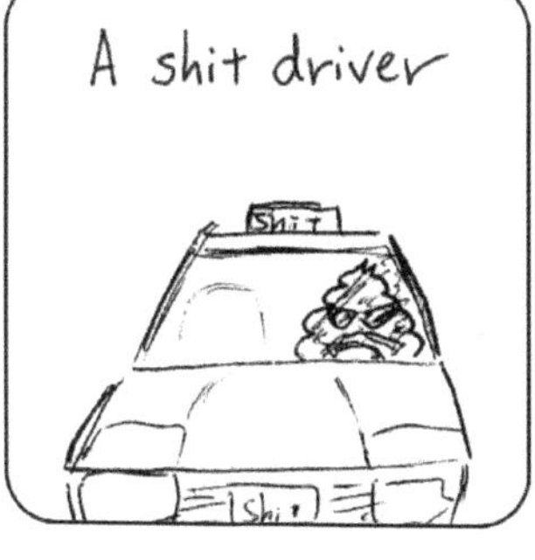
A shit driver
Shit
Shit

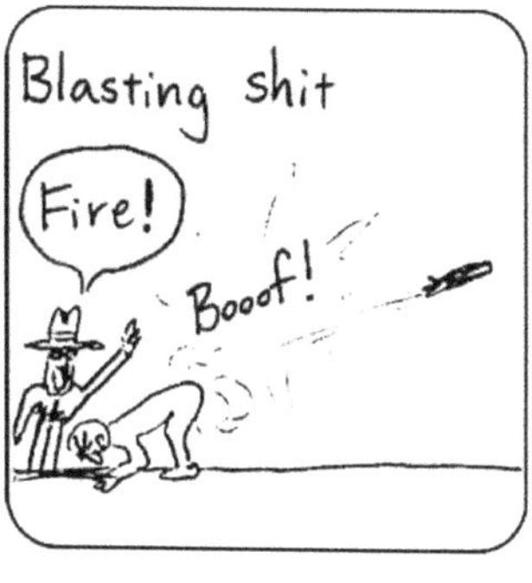
Blasting shit
Fire!
Booof!

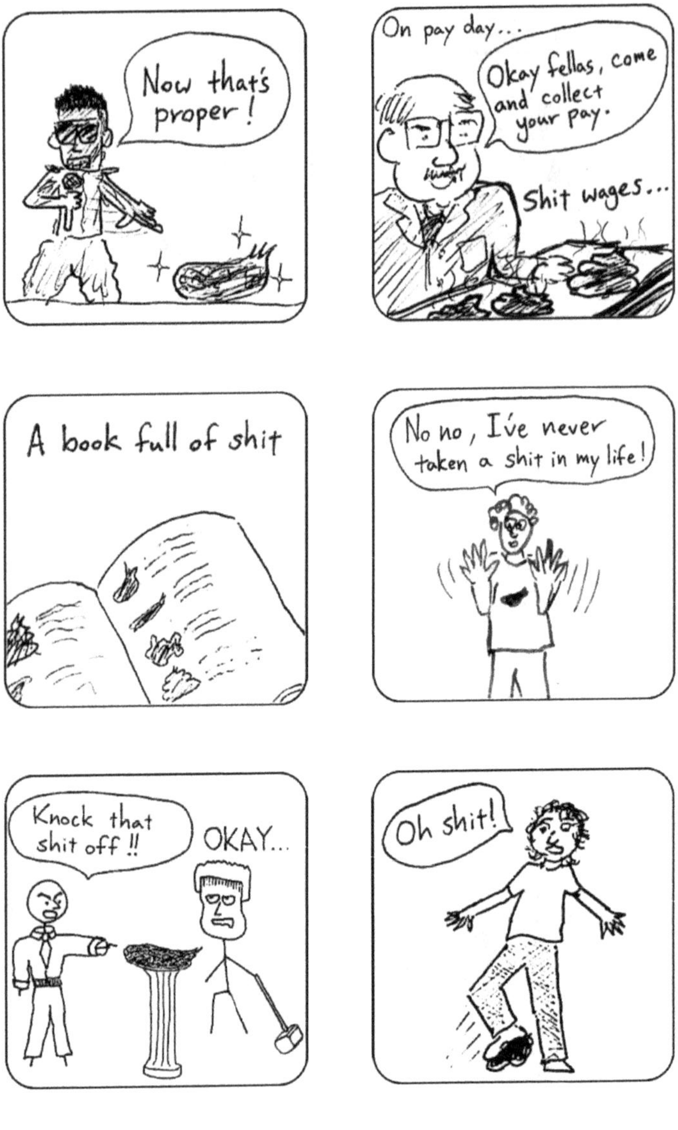
Now that's proper!
On pay day...
Okay fellas, come and collect your pay.
Shit wages...
A book full of shit
No no, I've never taken a shit in my life!
Knock that shit off !!
OKAY...
Oh shit!

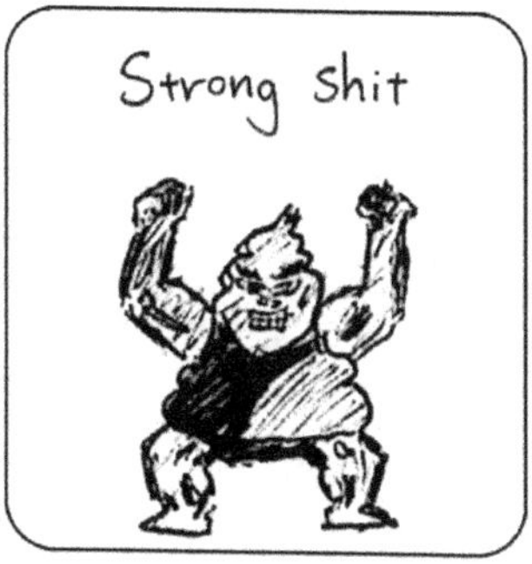
Strong shit

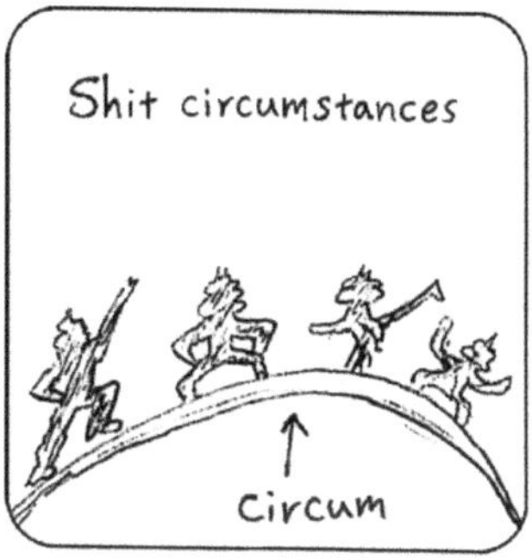
Shit circumstances
circum

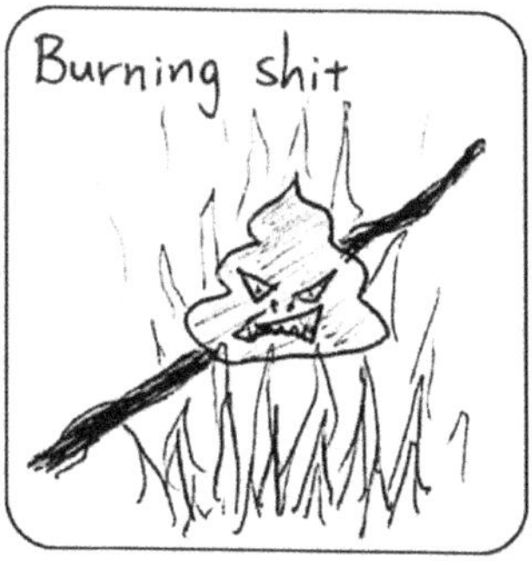
Burning shit

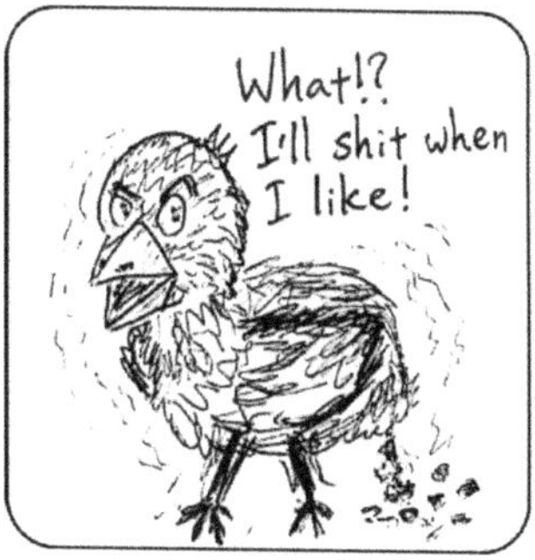
What!? I'll shit when I like!

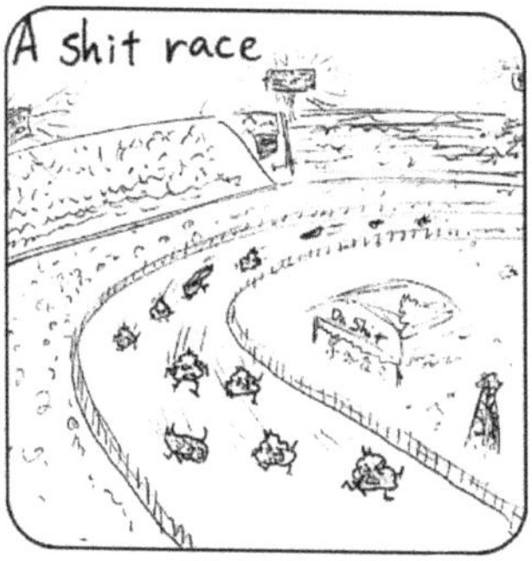
A shit race

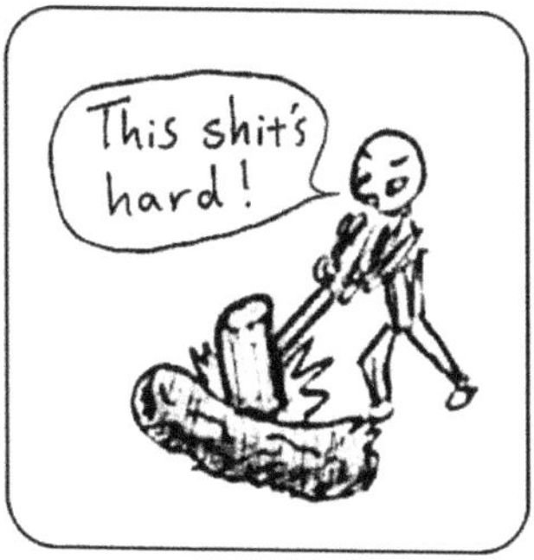
This shit's hard!

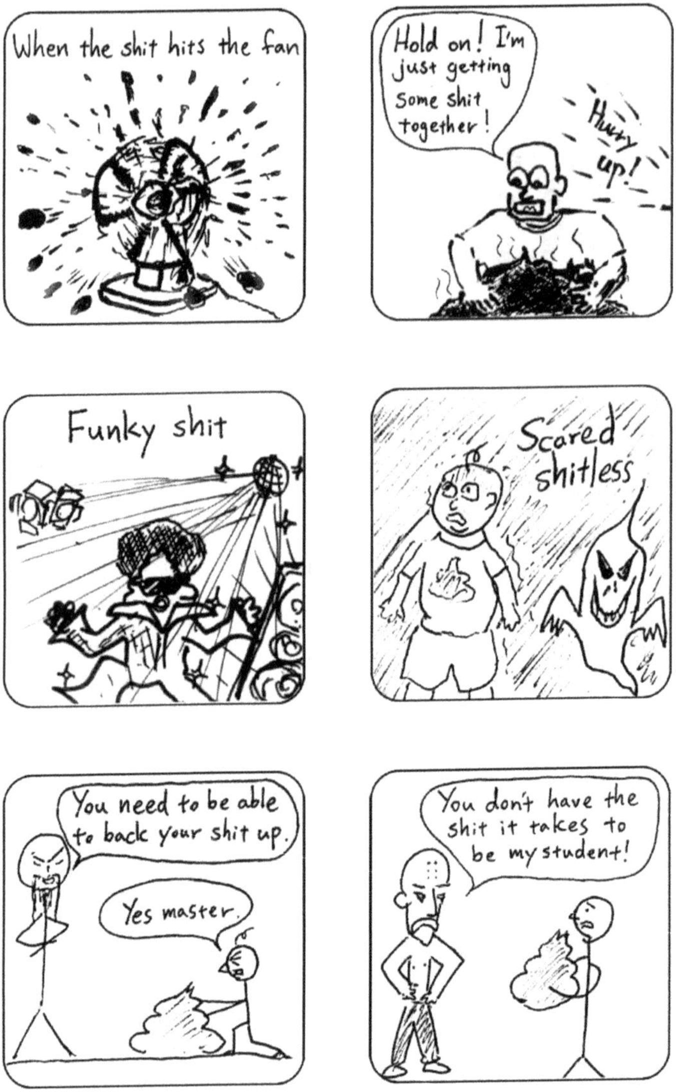
When the shit hits the fan
Hold on! I'm just getting some shit together!
Hurry up!
Funky shit
Scared shitless
You need to be able to back your shit up.
Yes master.
You don't have the shit it takes to be my student!

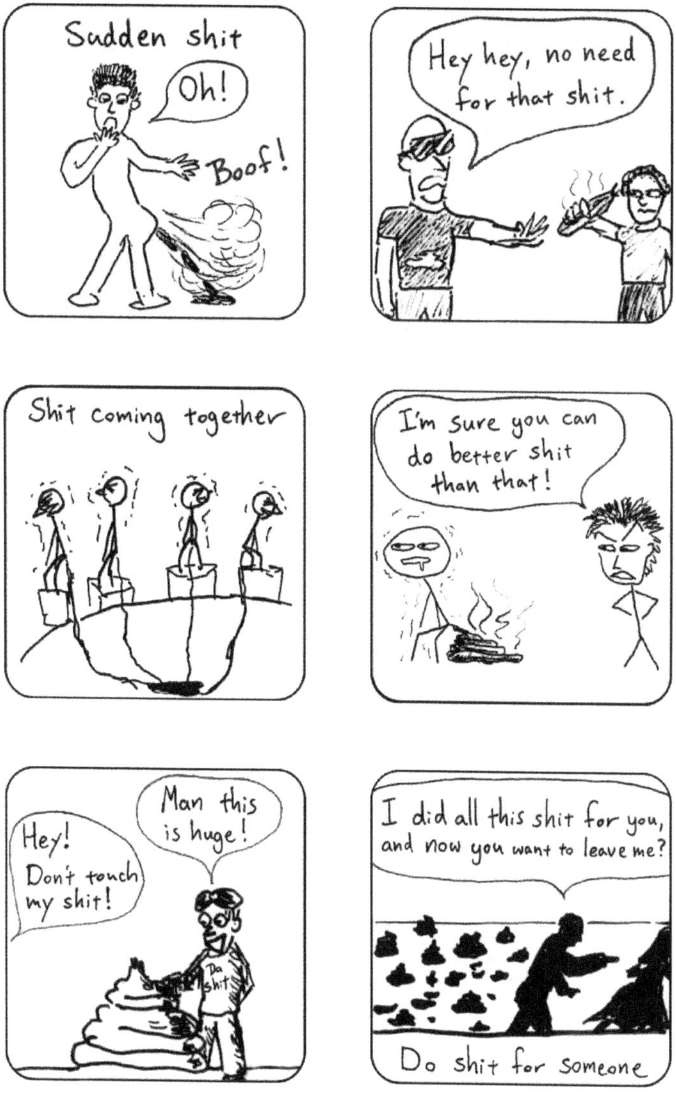
Sudden shit
Oh!
Boof!
Hey hey, no need for that shit.
Shit coming together
I'm sure you can do better shit than that!
Hey! Don't touch my shit!
Man this is huge!
Do shit
I did all this shit for you, and now you want to leave me?
Do shit for someone

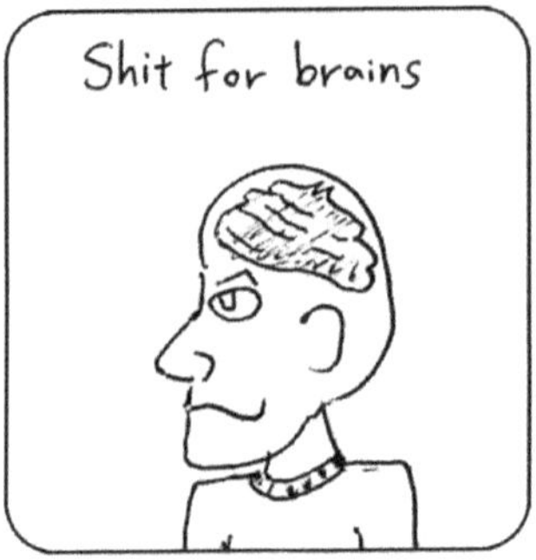
Shit for brains

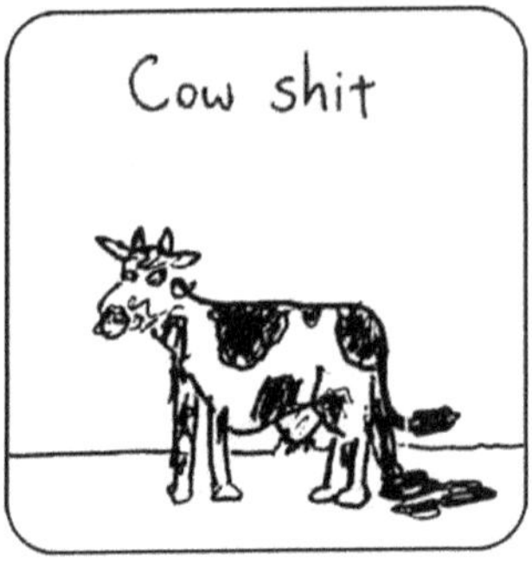
Cow shit

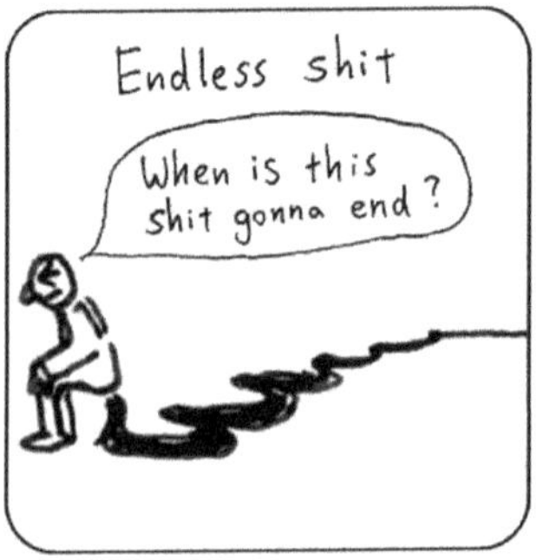
Endless shit
When is this shit gonna end ?

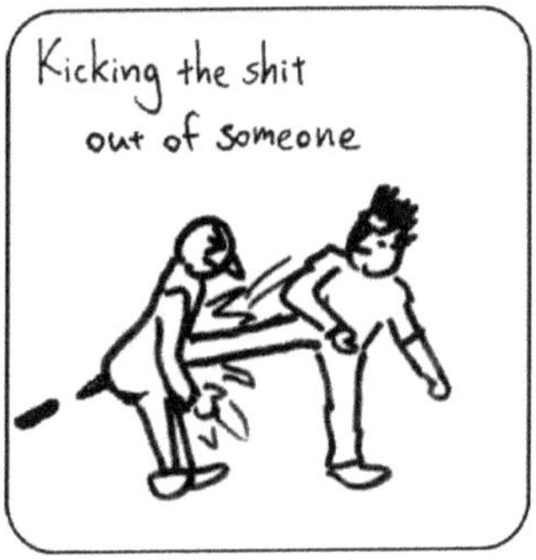
Kicking the shit out of someone

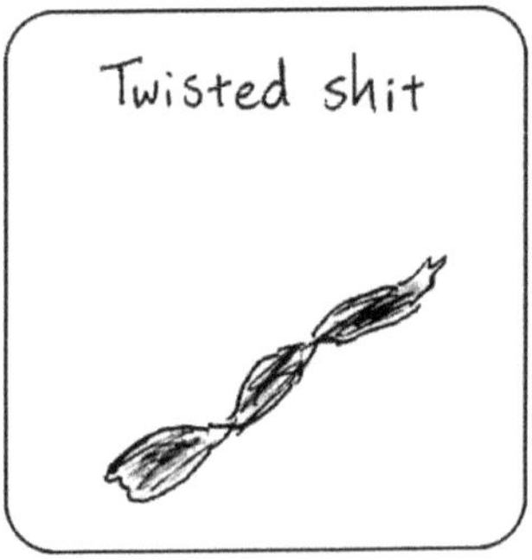
Twisted shit

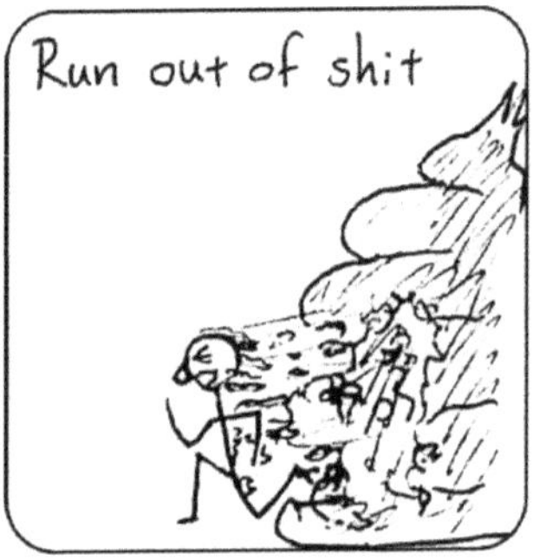
Run out of shit

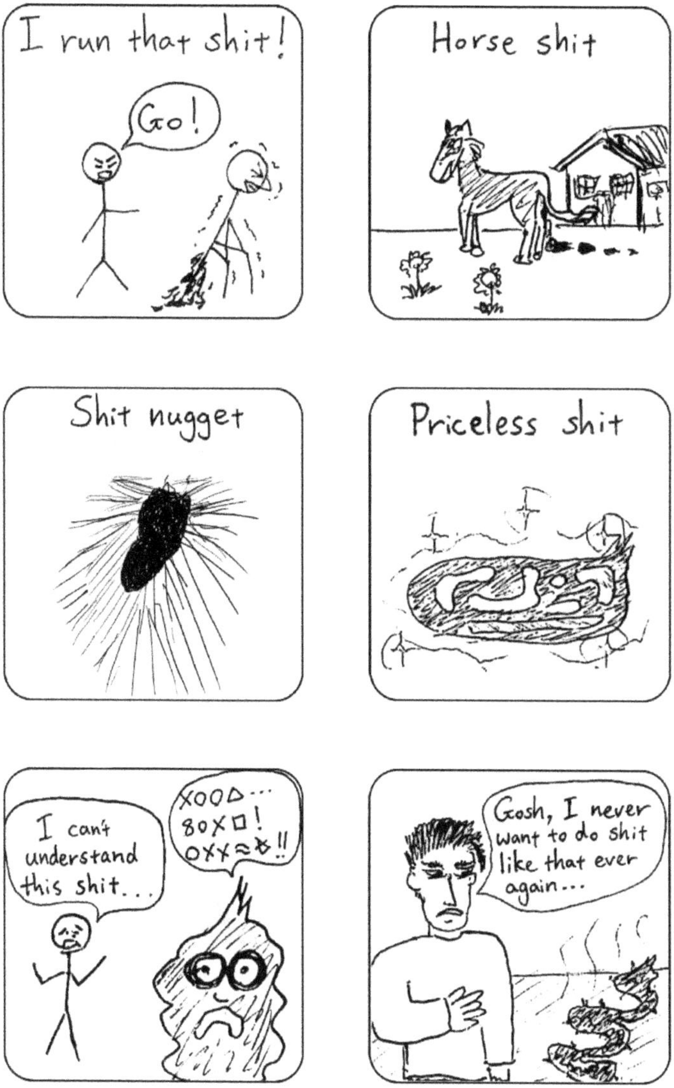
I run that shit!
Go!
Horse shit
Shit nugget
Priceless shit
I can't understand this shit...
Gosh, I never want to do shit like that ever again...

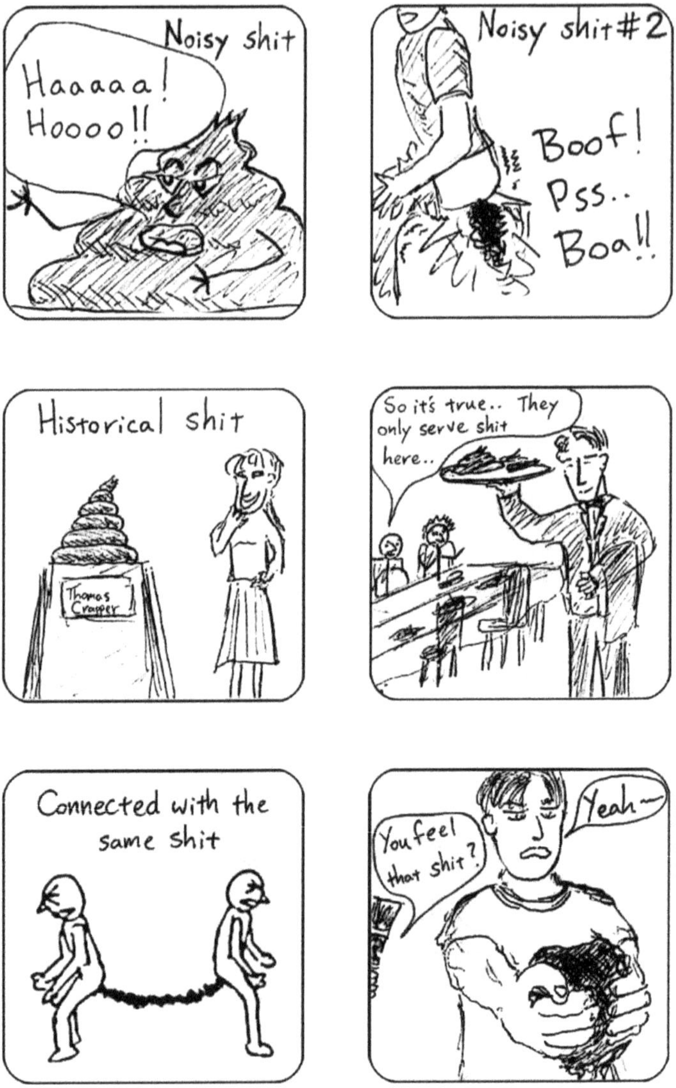
Noisy shit
Haaaaa! Hoooo!!
Noisy shit #2
Boof! Pss.. Boa!!
Historical shit
Thomas Crapper
So it's true.. They only serve shit here..
Connected with the same shit
You feel that shit?
Yeah~

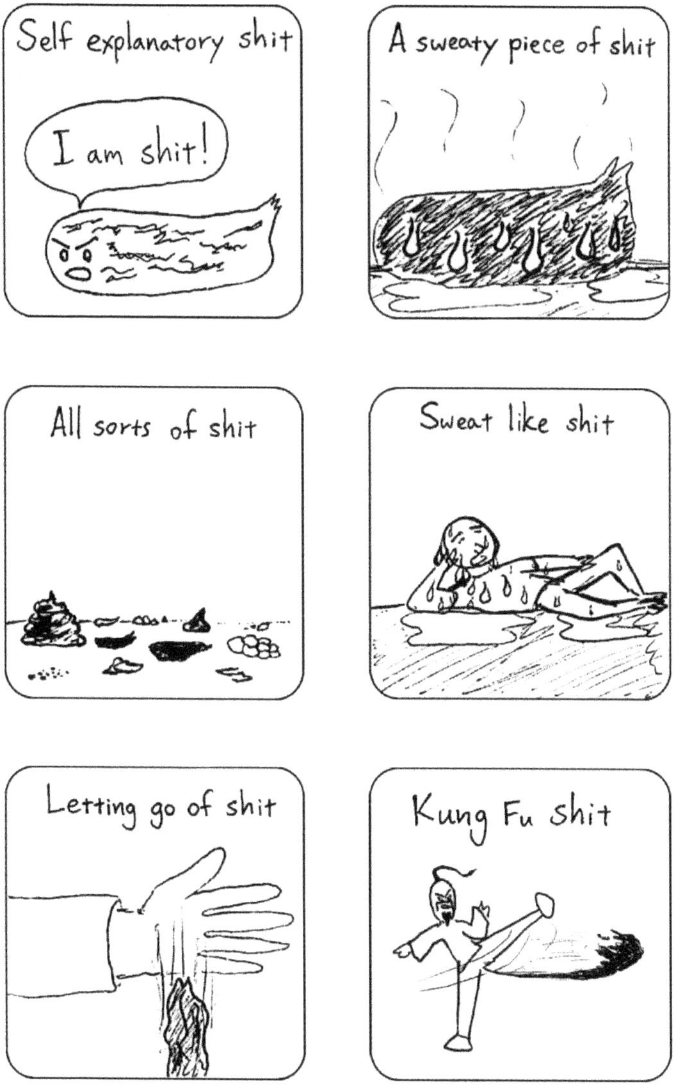
Self explanatory shit
I am shit!
A sweaty piece of shit
All sorts of shit
Sweat like shit
Letting go of shit
Kung Fu shit

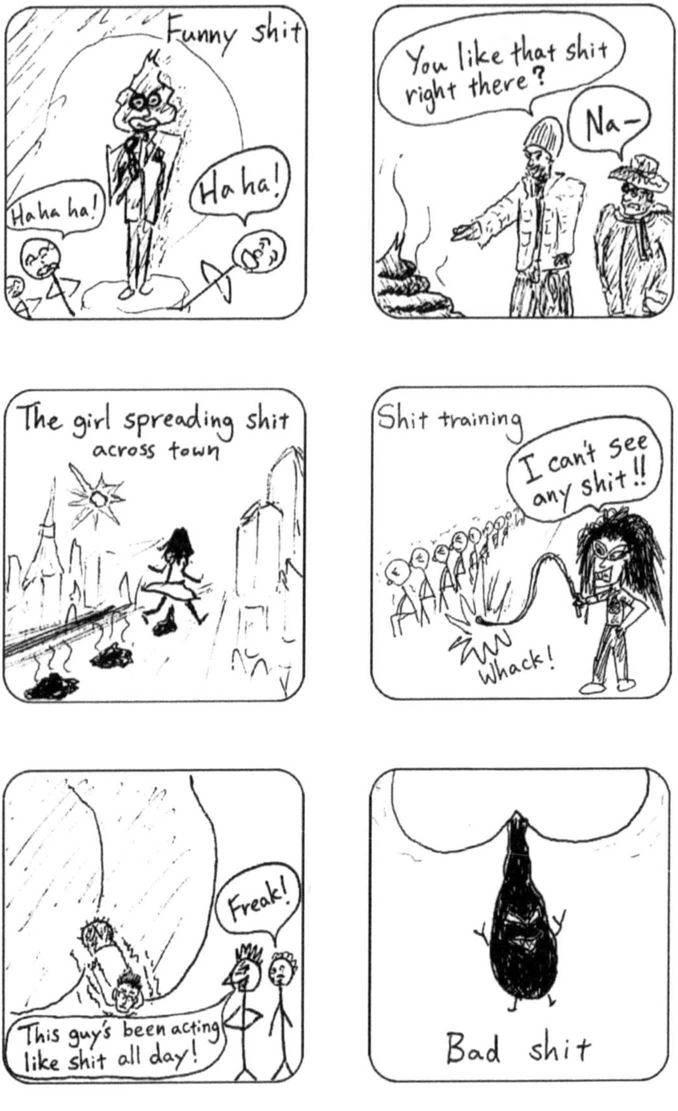
Funny shit
Haha ha!
Ha ha!
You like that shit right there?
Na-
The girl spreading shit across town
Shit training
I can't see any shit!!
Whack!
Freak!
This guy's been acting like shit all day!
Bad shit

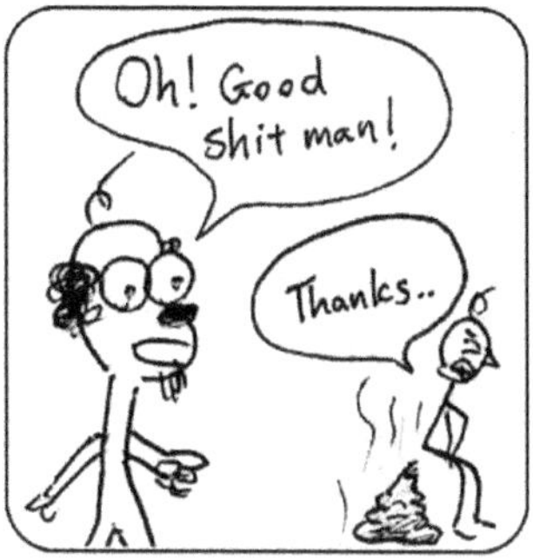
Oh! Good shit man!
Thanks..

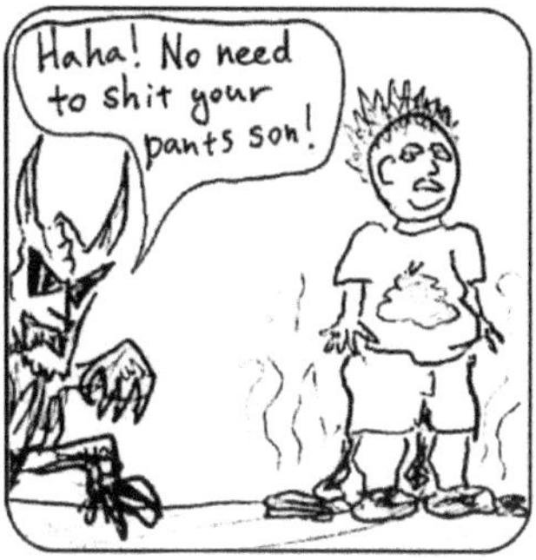
Haha! No need to shit your pants son!

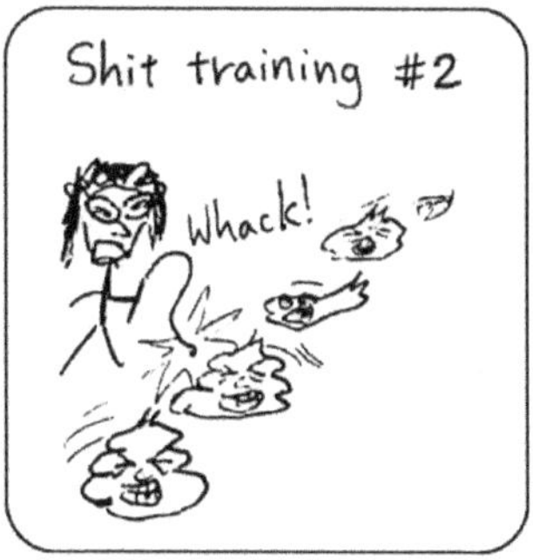
Shit training #2
Whack!

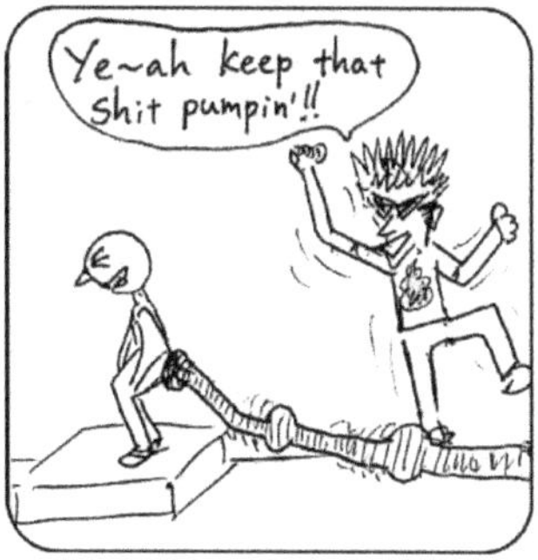
Ye~ah keep that shit pumpin'!!

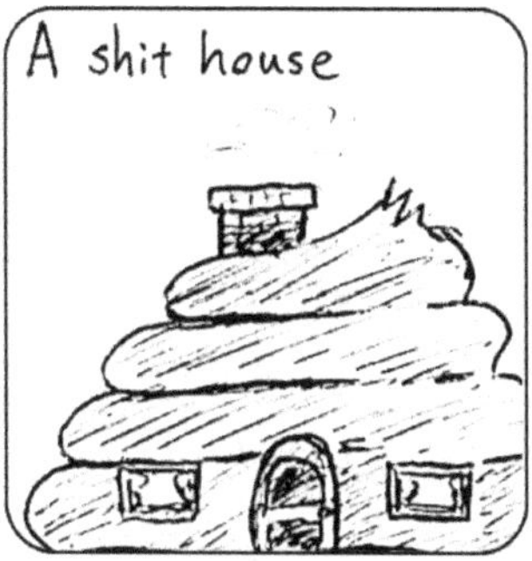
A shit house

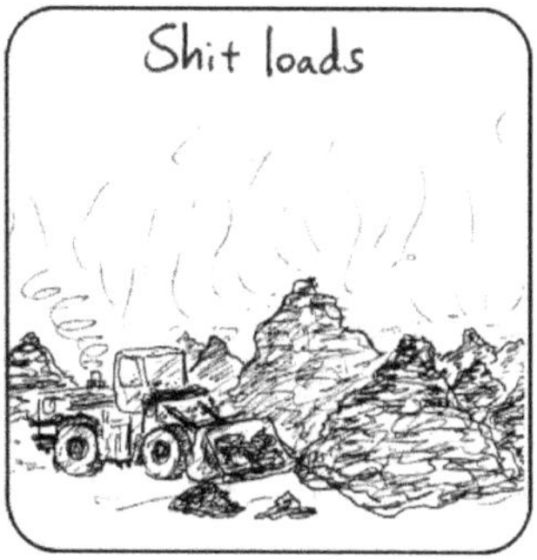
Shit loads

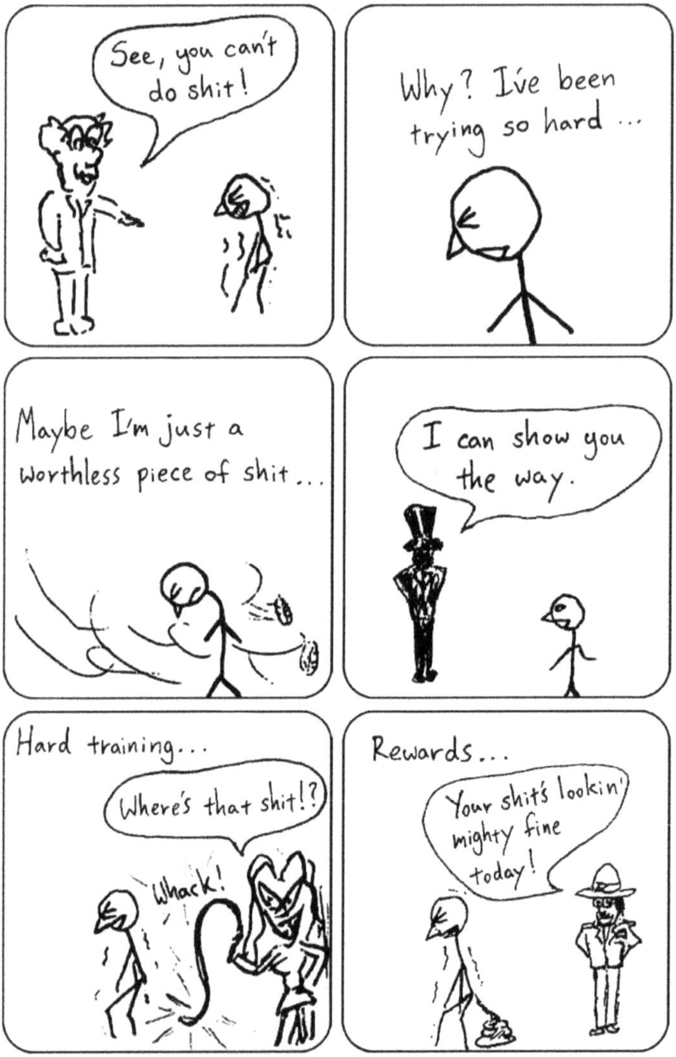
See, you can't do shit!
Why? I've been trying so hard ...
Maybe I'm just a worthless piece of shit ...
I can show you the way.
Hard training...
Where's that shit!?
Whack!
Rewards...
Your shit's lookin' mighty fine today!

2

Taking it further

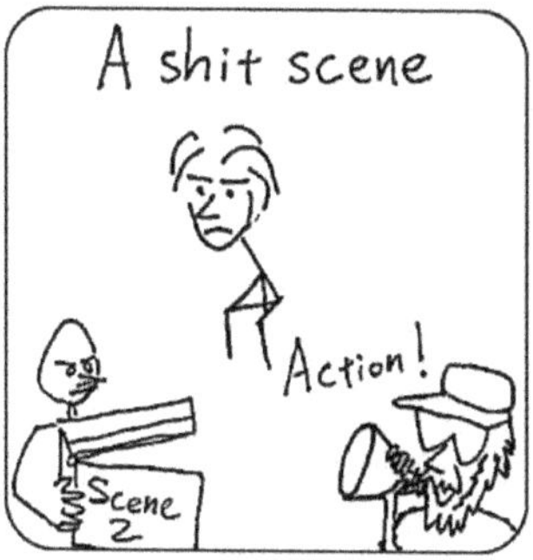
A shit scene
Action!
Scene 2

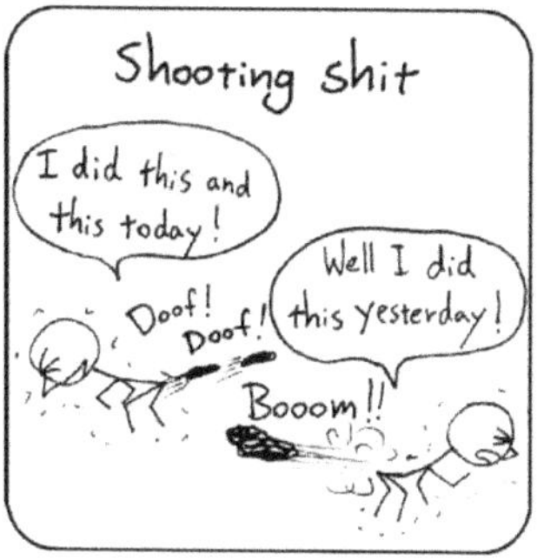
Shooting shit
I did this and this today!
Well I did this yesterday!
Doof!
Doof!
Booom!!

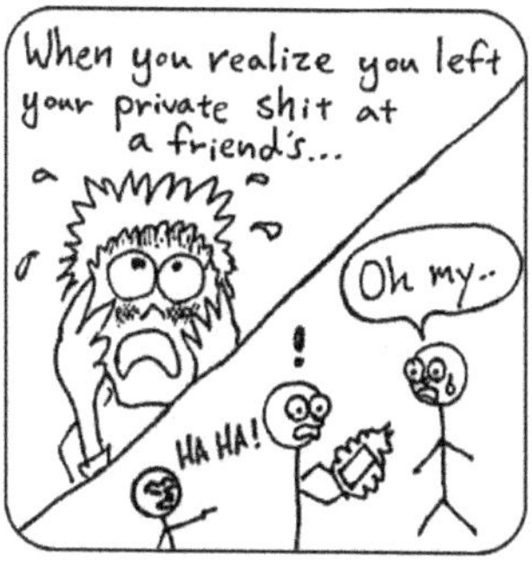
When you realize you left your private shit at a friend's...
Oh my..
!
HA HA!

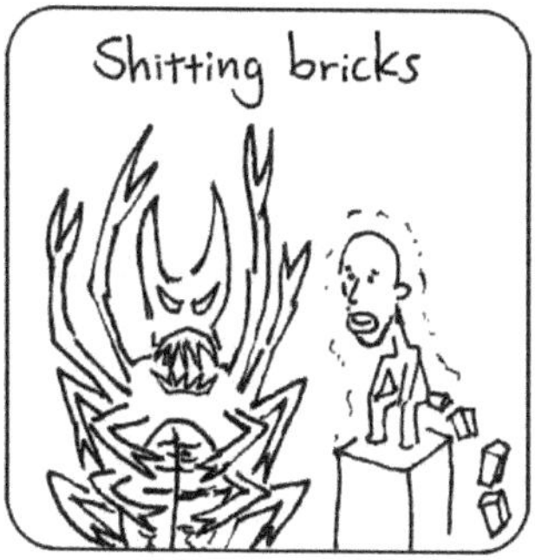
Shitting bricks

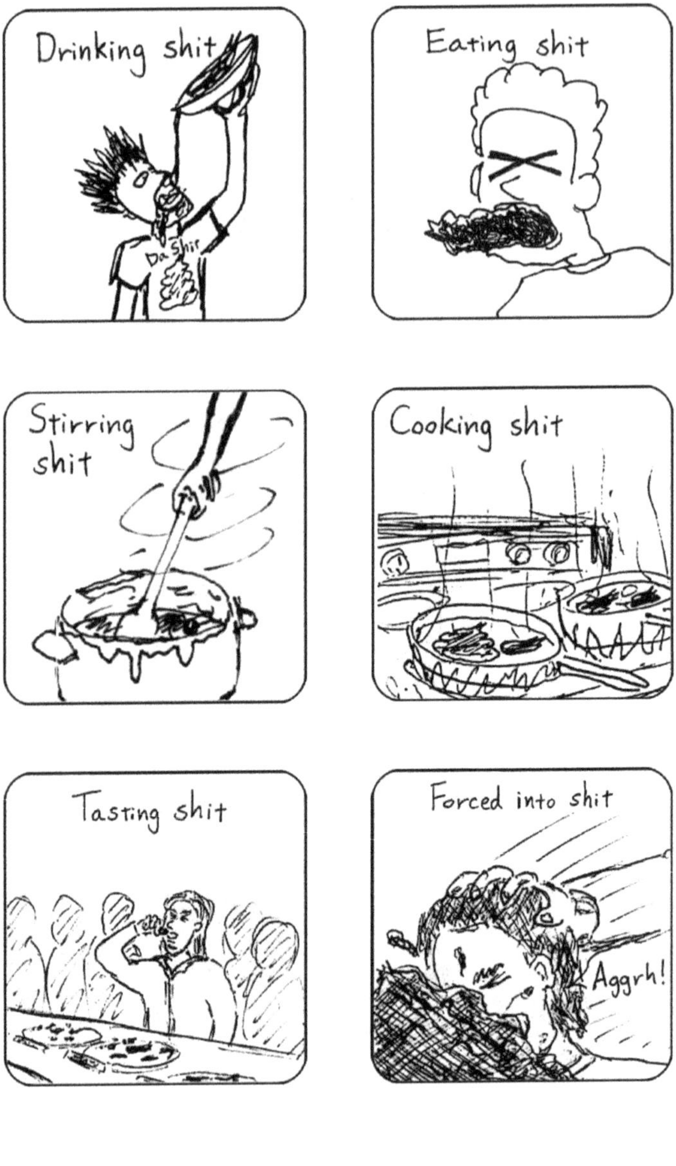
Drinking shit
Eating shit
Stirring shit
Cooking shit
Tasting shit
Forced into shit
Aggrh!

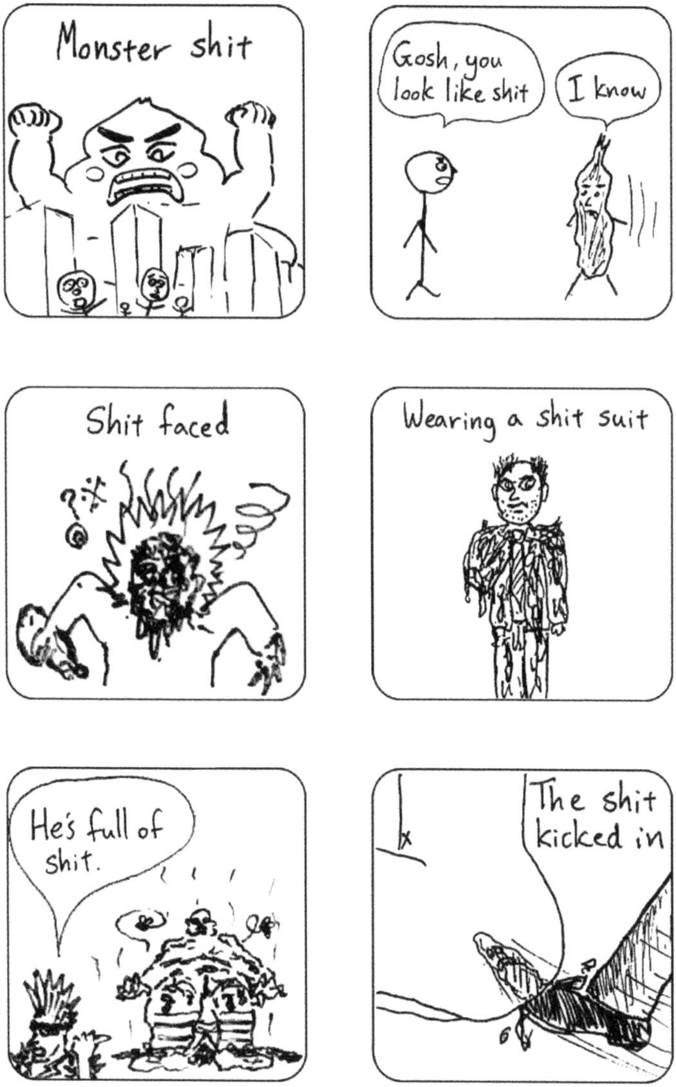
Monster shit
Gosh, you look like shit
I know
Shit faced
Wearing a shit suit
He's full of shit.
The shit kicked in

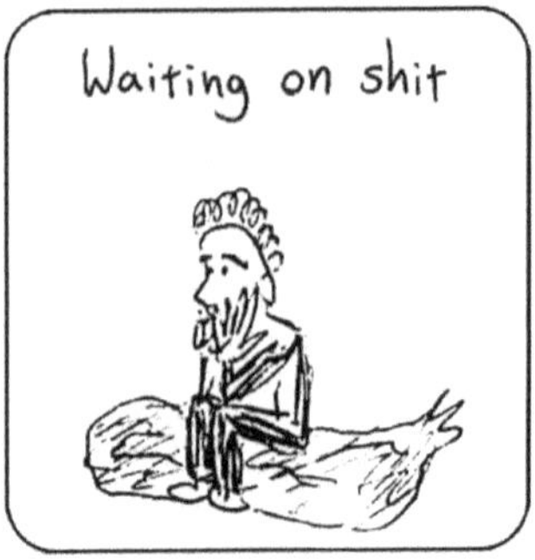
Waiting on shit

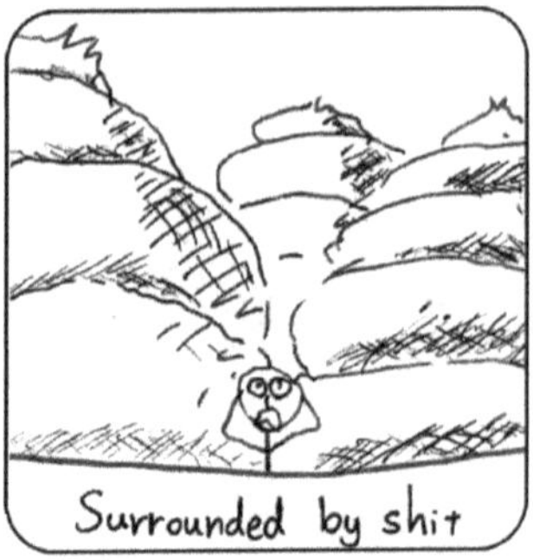
Surrounded by shit

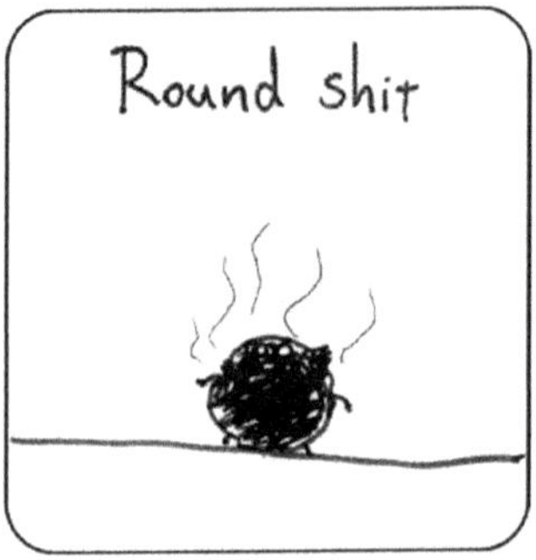
Round shit

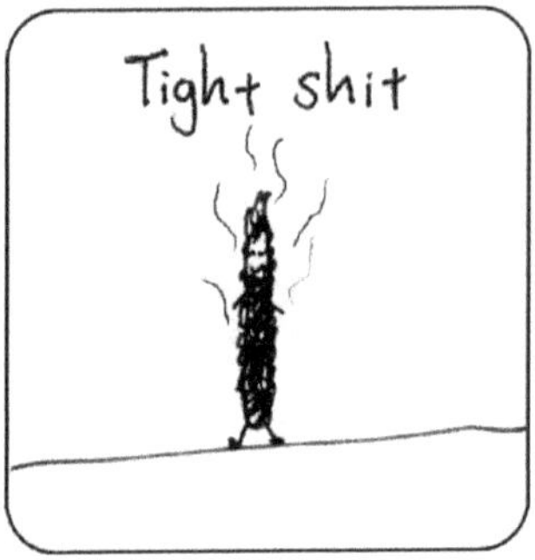
Tight shit

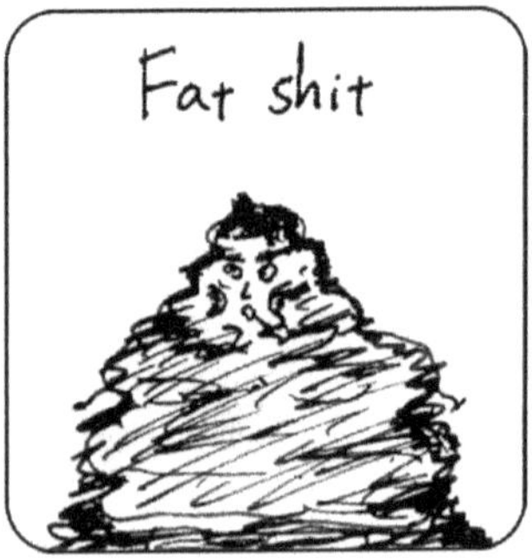
Fat shit

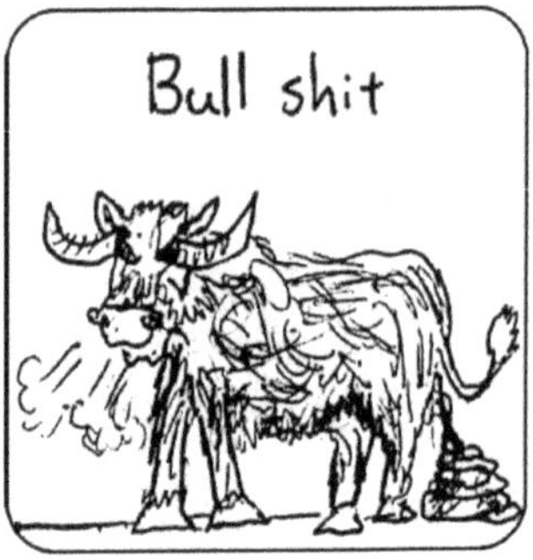
Bull shit

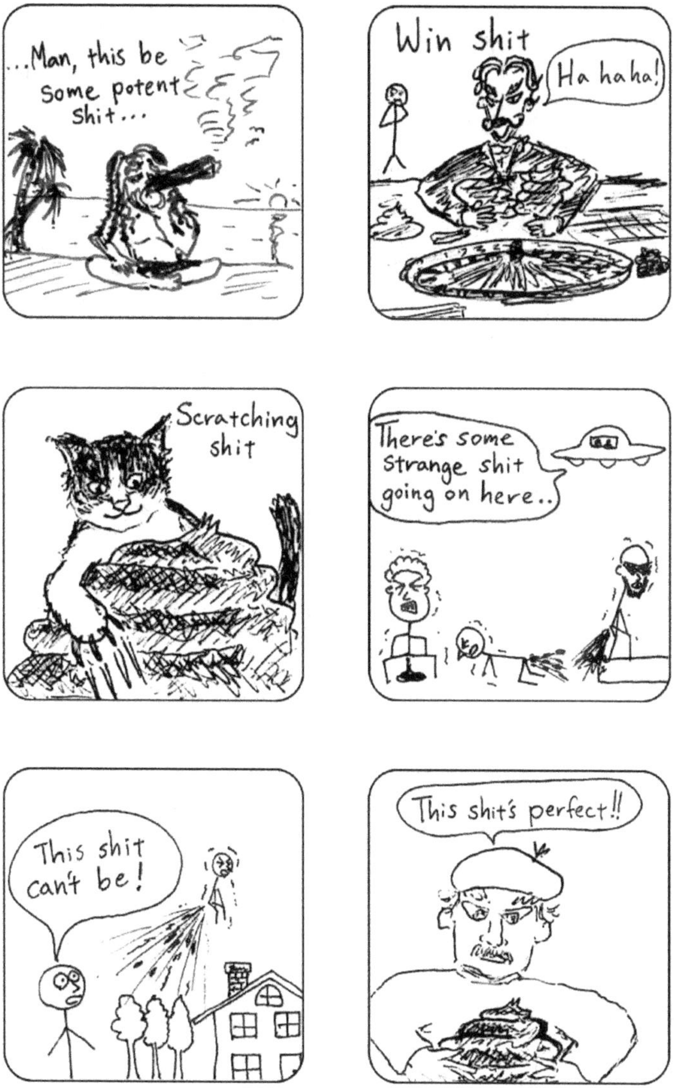
...Man, this be some potent shit...
Win shit
Ha haha!
Scratching shit
There's some strange shit going on here..
This shit can't be!
This shit's perfect!!

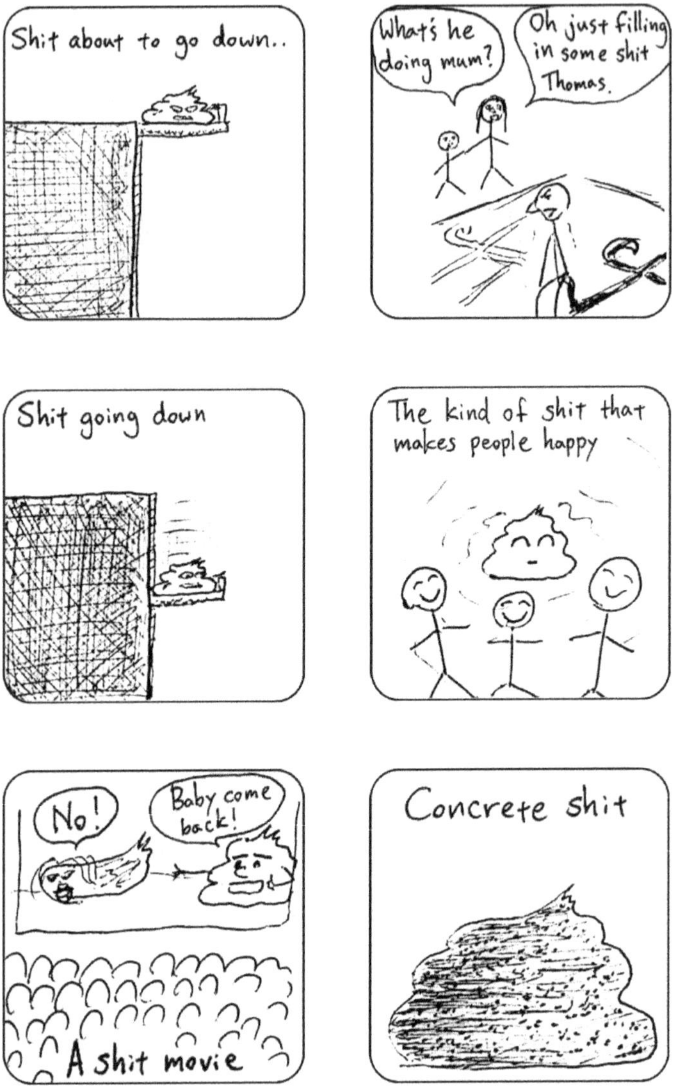
Shit about to go down..
What's he doing mum?
Oh just filling in some shit Thomas.
Shit going down
The kind of shit that makes people happy
No!
Baby come back!
A shit movie
Concrete shit

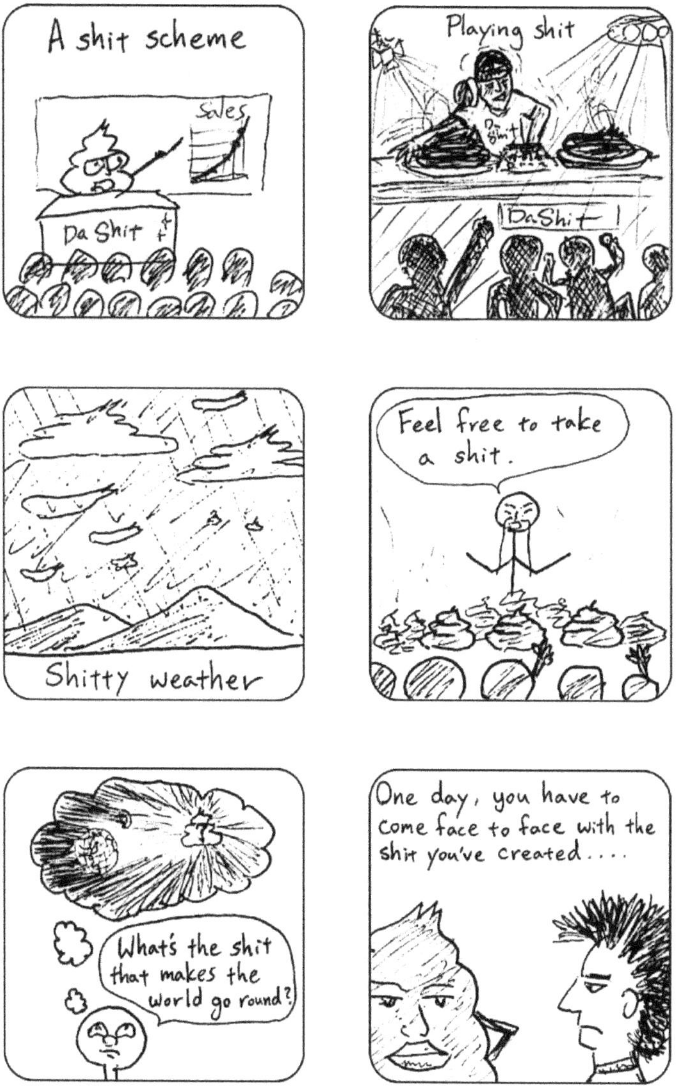
A shit scheme
Sales
Da Shit
Playing shit
DaShit
Shitty weather
Feel free to take a shit.
What's the shit that makes the world go round?
One day, you have to come face to face with the shit you've created....

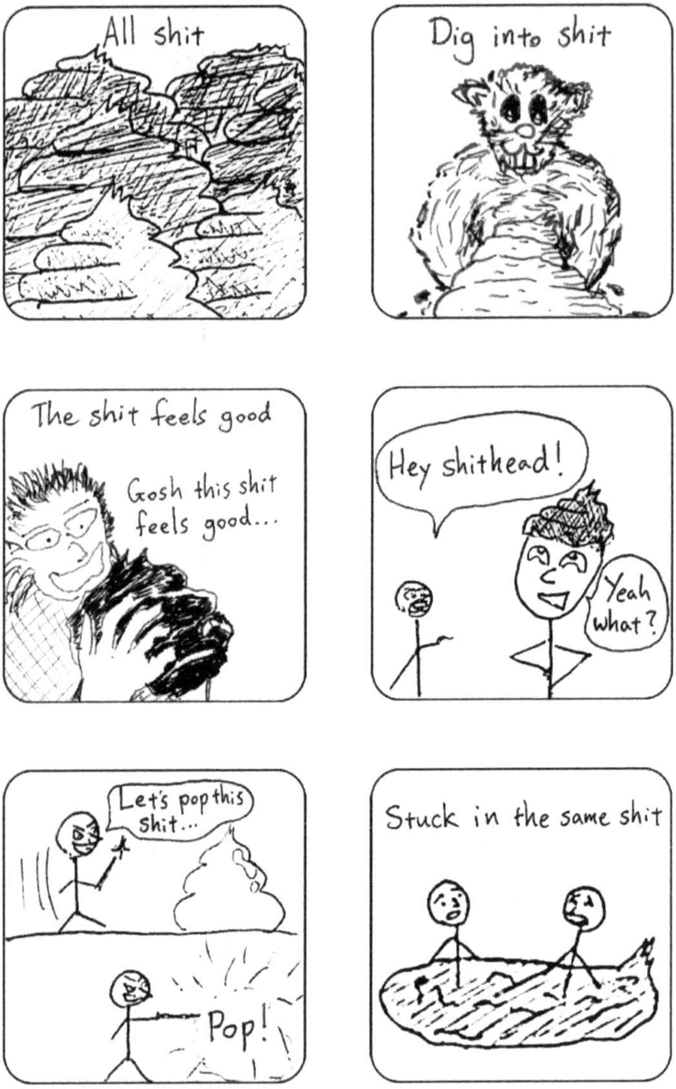
All shit
Dig into shit
The shit feels good
Gosh this shit feels good...
Hey shithead!
Yeah what?
Let's pop this shit...
Pop!
Stuck in the same shit

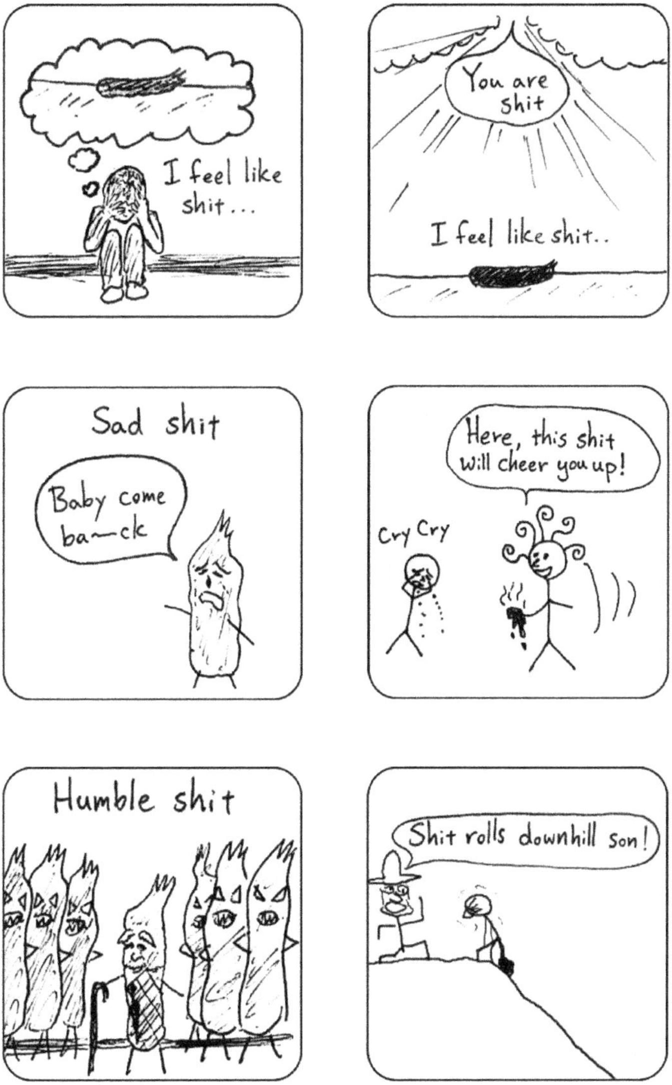
I feel like shit...
You are shit
I feel like shit..
Sad shit
Baby come ba~ck
Here, this shit will cheer you up!
Cry Cry
Humble shit
Shit rolls downhill son!

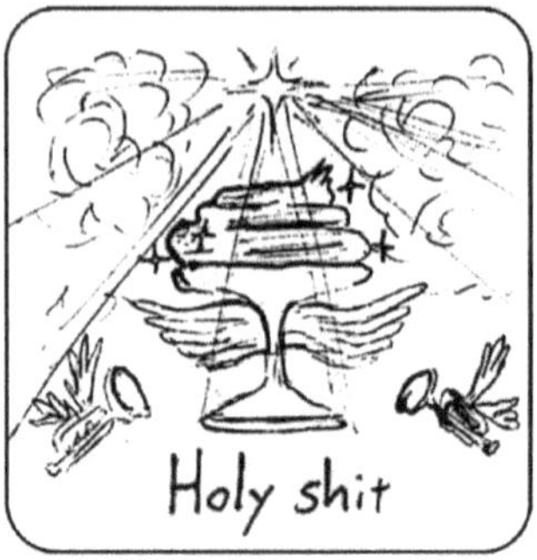
Holy shit

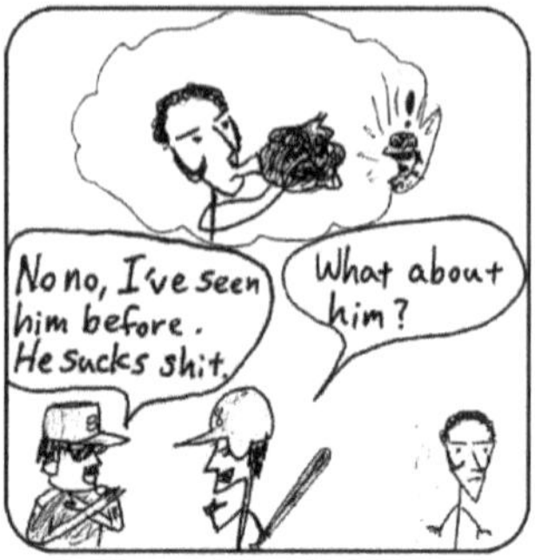
No no, I've seen him before. He sucks shit.
What about him?

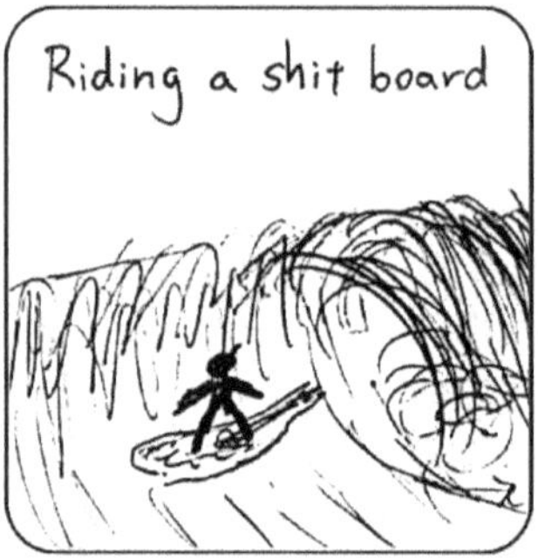
Riding a shit board

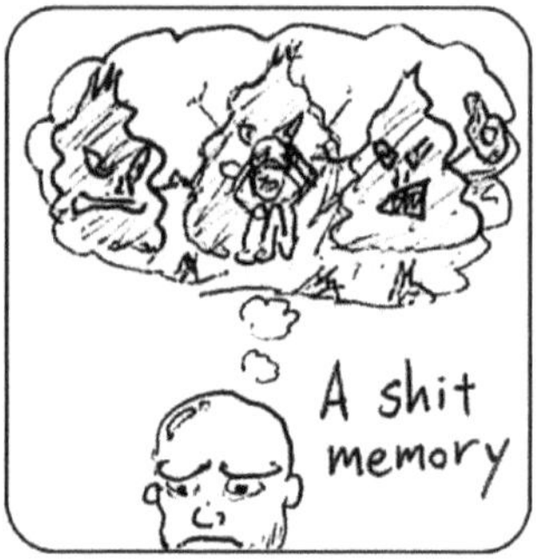
A shit memory

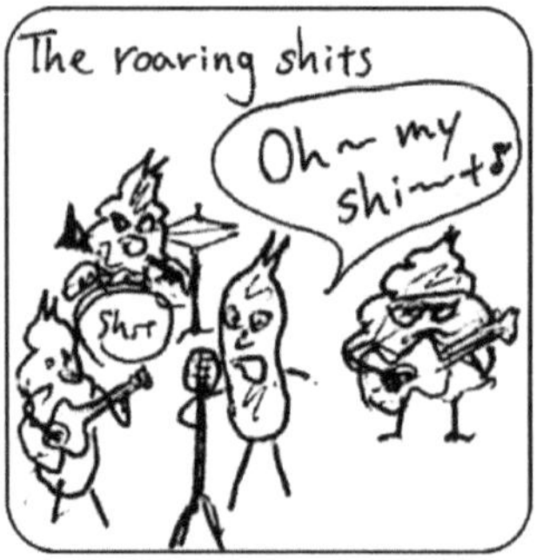
The roaring shits
Oh~ my shi~t
Shit

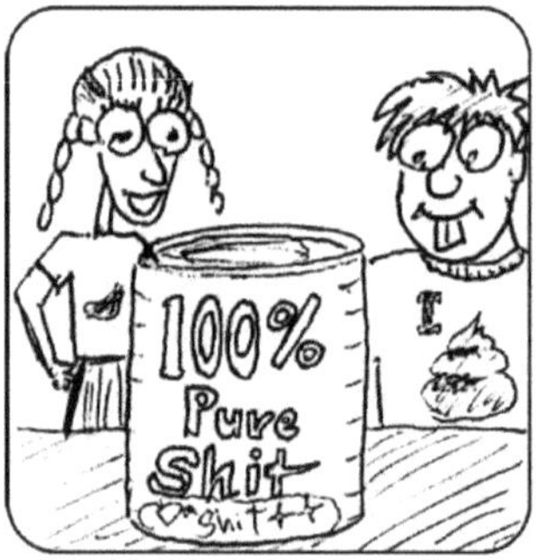
100% Pure Shit
I

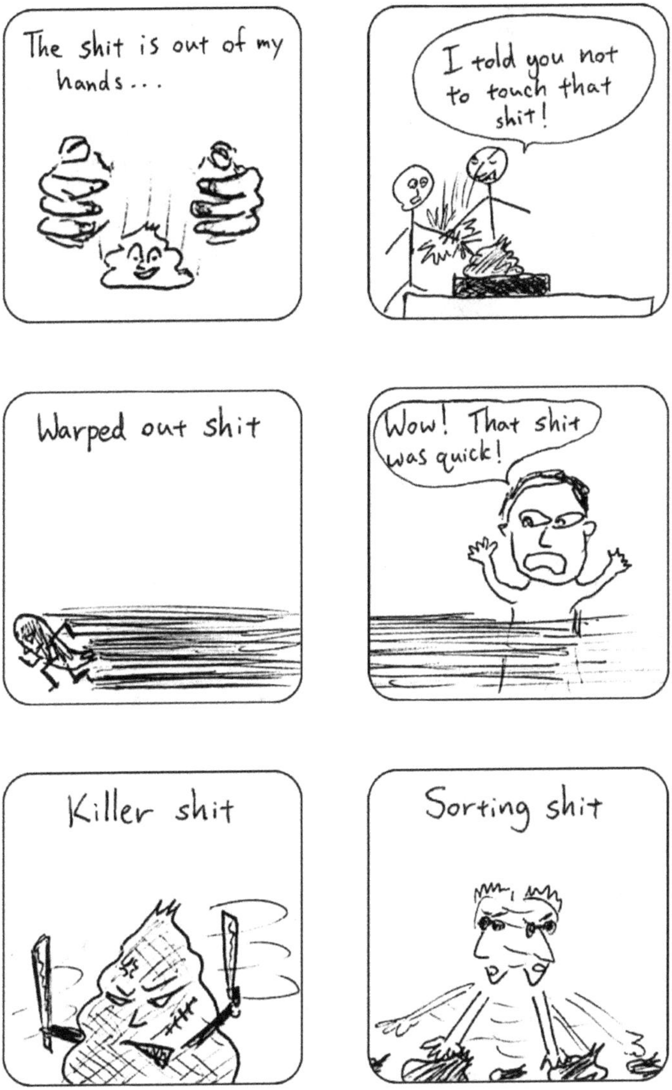
The shit is out of my hands...
I told you not to touch that shit!
Warped out shit
Wow! That shit was quick!
Killer shit
Sorting shit

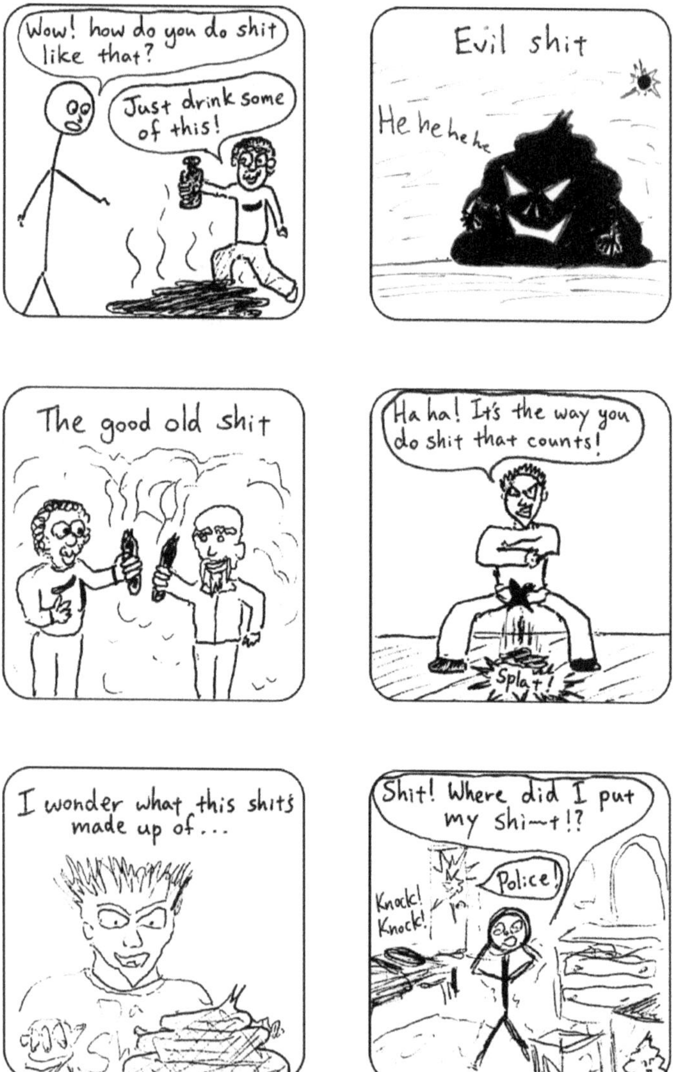
Wow! how do you do shit like that?
Just drink some of this!
Evil shit
He he he he
The good old shit
Ha ha! It's the way you do shit that counts!
Splat!
I wonder what this shit's made up of...
Shit! Where did I put my shi—t!?
Knock! Knock!
Police!

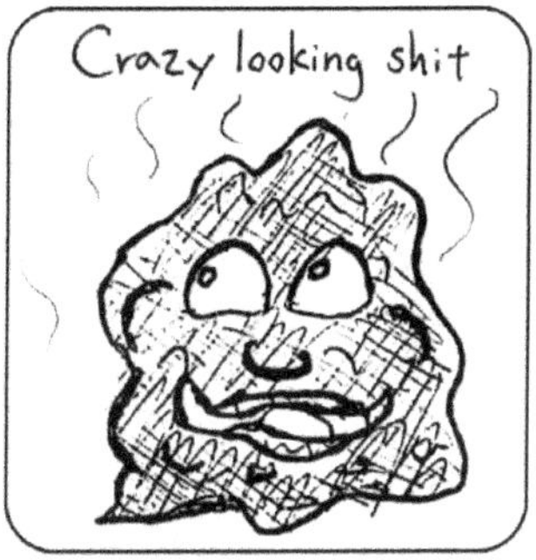
Crazy looking shit

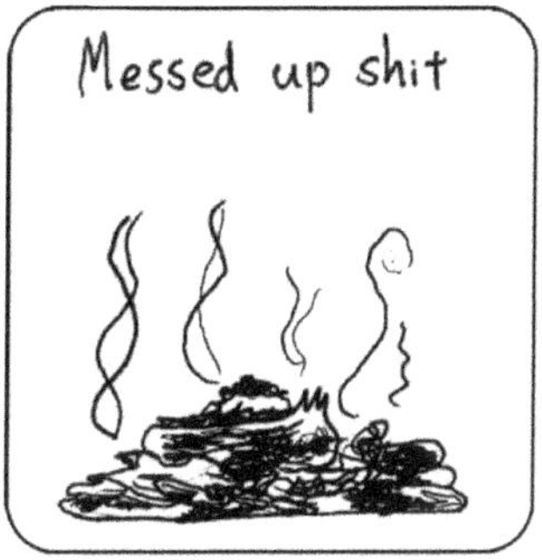
Messed up shit

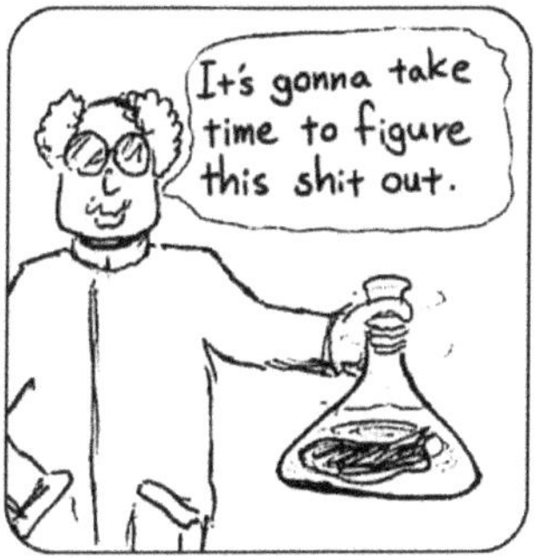
It's gonna take time to figure this shit out.

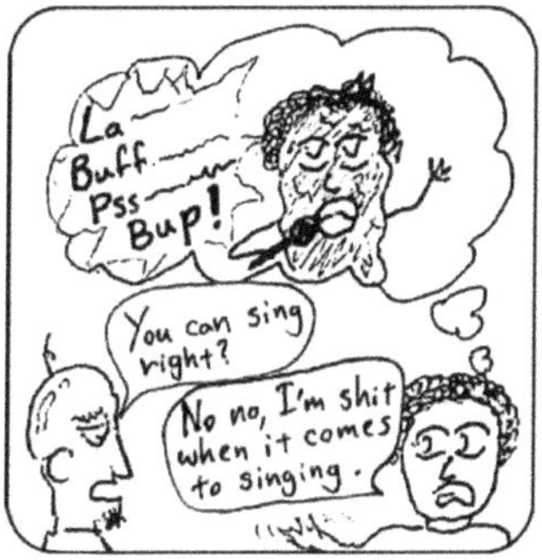
La
Buff
Pss
Bup!
You can sing right?
No no, I'm shit when it comes to singing.

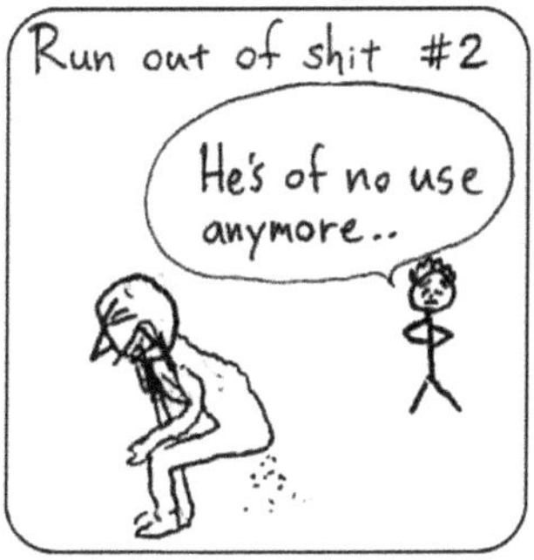
Run out of shit #2
He's of no use anymore..

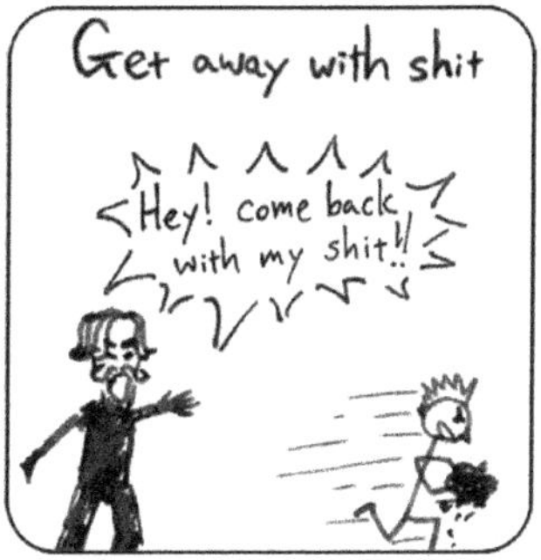
Get away with shit
Hey! come back with my shit!!

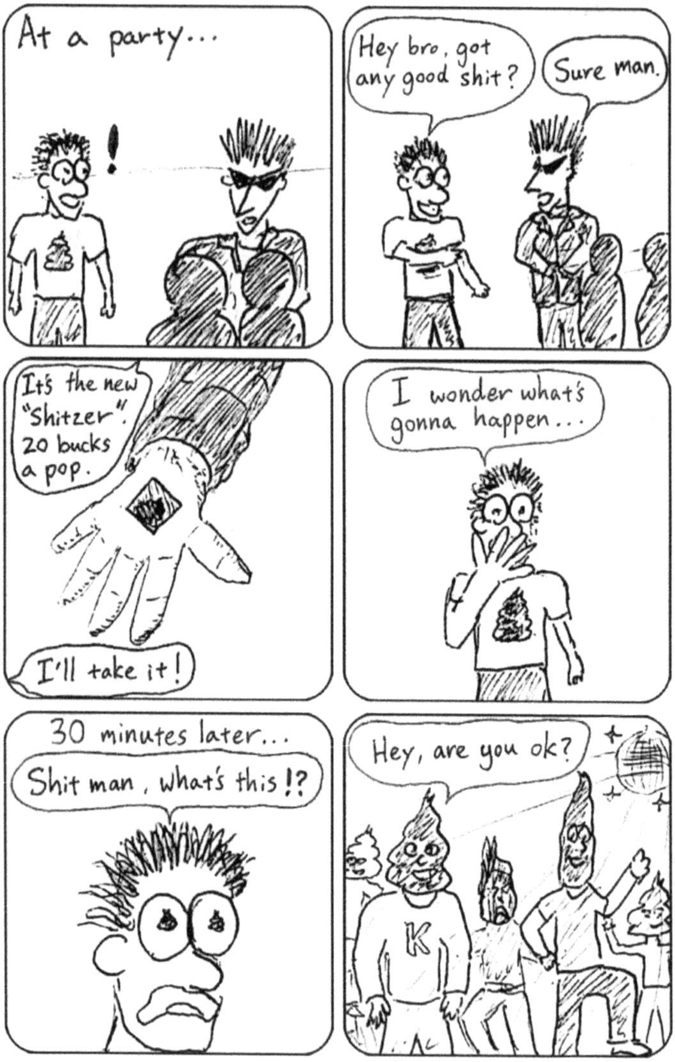
At a party...
!
Hey bro, got any good shit?
Sure man.
It's the new "Shitzer". 20 bucks a pop.
I'll take it!
I wonder what's gonna happen...
30 minutes later...
Shit man, what's this!?
Hey, are you ok?
K

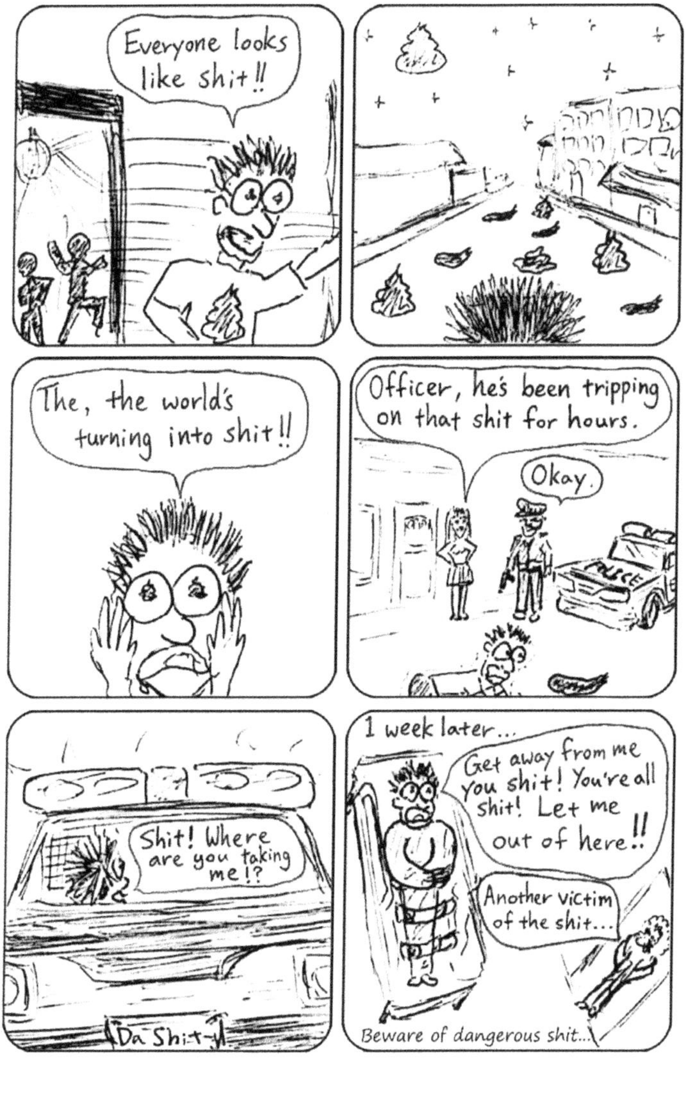
Everyone looks like shit!!
The, the world's turning into shit!!
Officer, he's been tripping on that shit for hours.
Okay.
POLICE
Shit! Where are you taking me!?
Da Shit
1 week later...
Get away from me you shit! You're all shit! Let me out of here!!
Another victim of the shit...
Beware of dangerous shit...

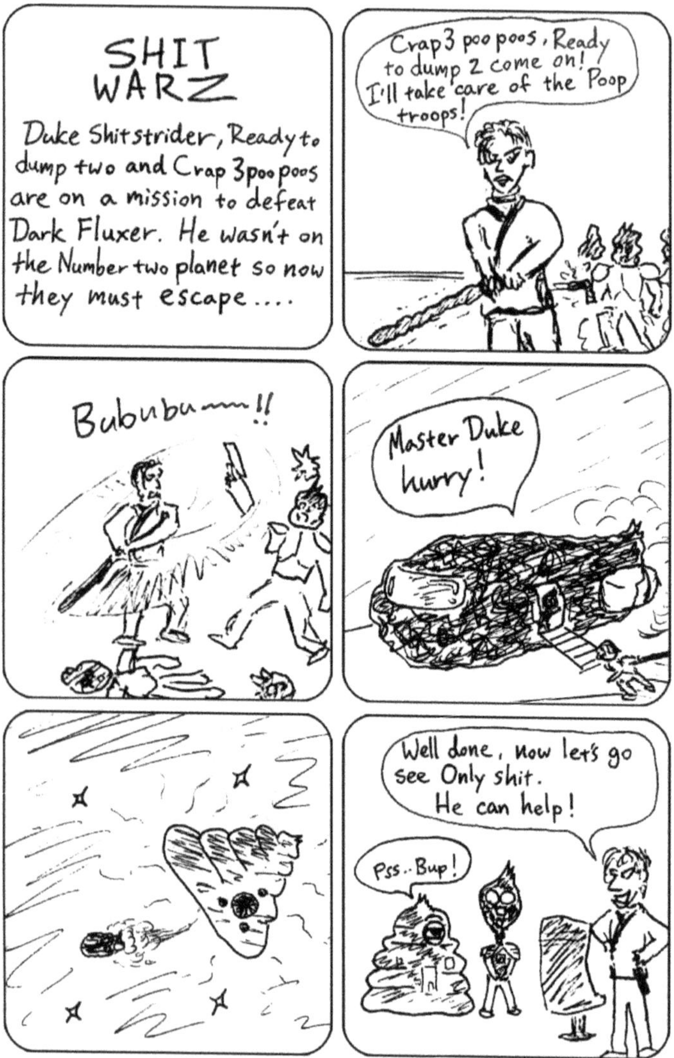
SHIT WARZ
Duke Shitstrider, Ready to dump two and Crap 3poo poos are on a mission to defeat Dark Fluxer. He wasn't on the Number two planet so now they must escape....
Crap3 poo poos, Ready to dump 2 come on! I'll take care of the Poop troops!
Bubububu~~~!!
Master Duke hurry!
Well done, now let's go see Only shit. He can help!
Pss.. Bup!

2 of 2 on page 64

3

Recognizing shit

Bro forget that shit.
I, I know this shit's gonna sound weird but...
Bubu!
Bzz.. Pss..
Boaabfzzsh!
Sucking shit out
Shit for shit

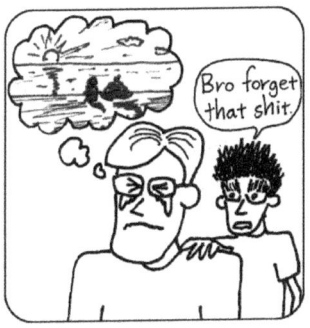

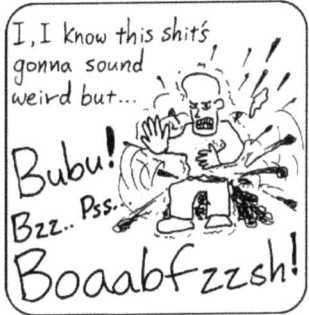

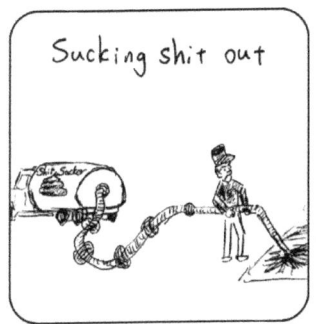

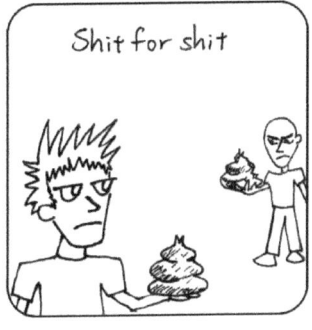

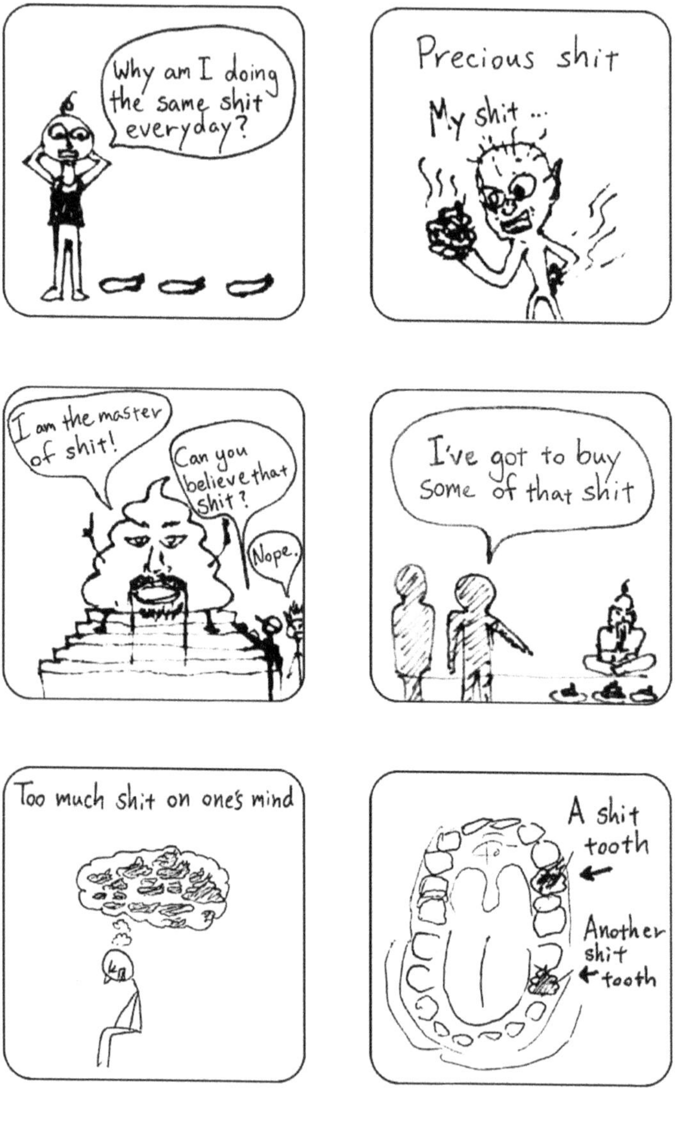
Why am I doing the same shit everyday?
Precious shit
My shit ...
I am the master of shit!
Can you believe that shit?
Nope.
I've got to buy some of that shit
Too much shit on one's mind
A shit tooth
Another shit tooth

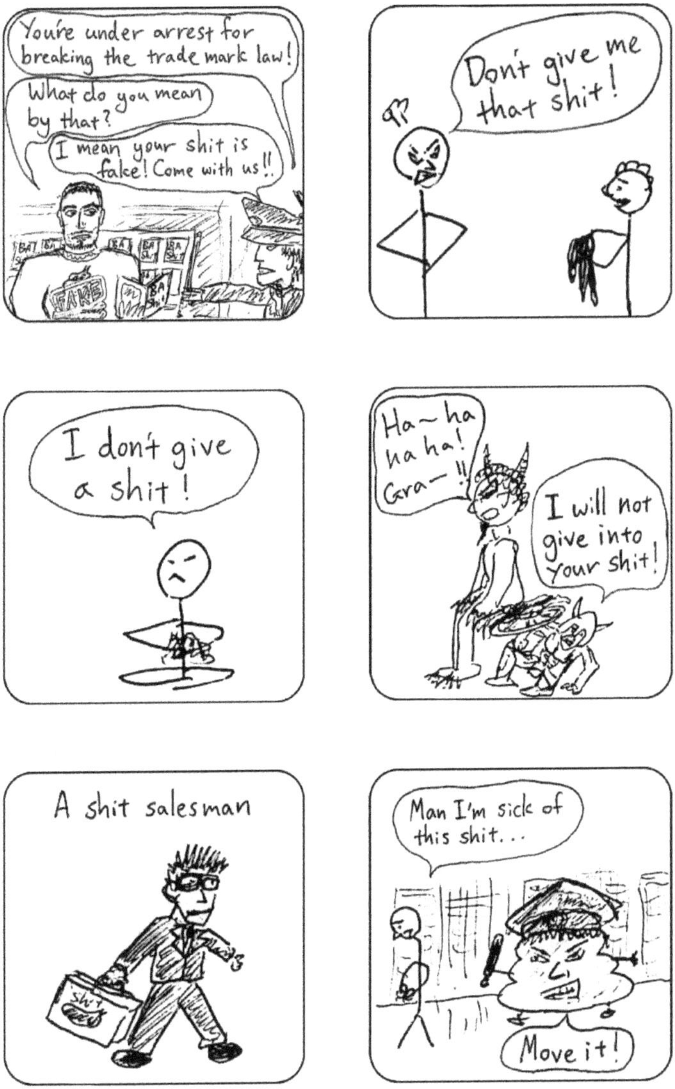
You're under arrest for breaking the trade mark law!
What do you mean by that?
I mean your shit is fake! Come with us!!
FAKE
Don't give me that shit!
I don't give a shit!
Ha~ha ha ha! Gra~!!
I will not give into your shit!
A shit salesman
Man I'm sick of this shit...
Move it!

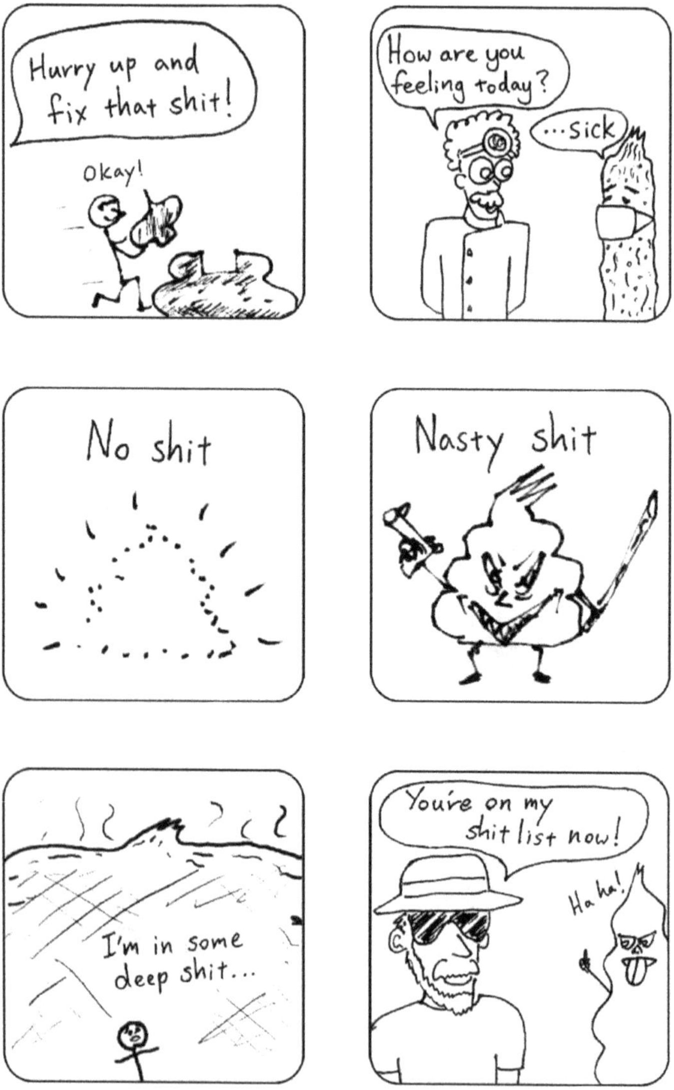
Hurry up and fix that shit!
Okay!
How are you feeling today?
...sick
No shit
Nasty shit
I'm in some deep shit...
You're on my shit list now!
Ha ha!

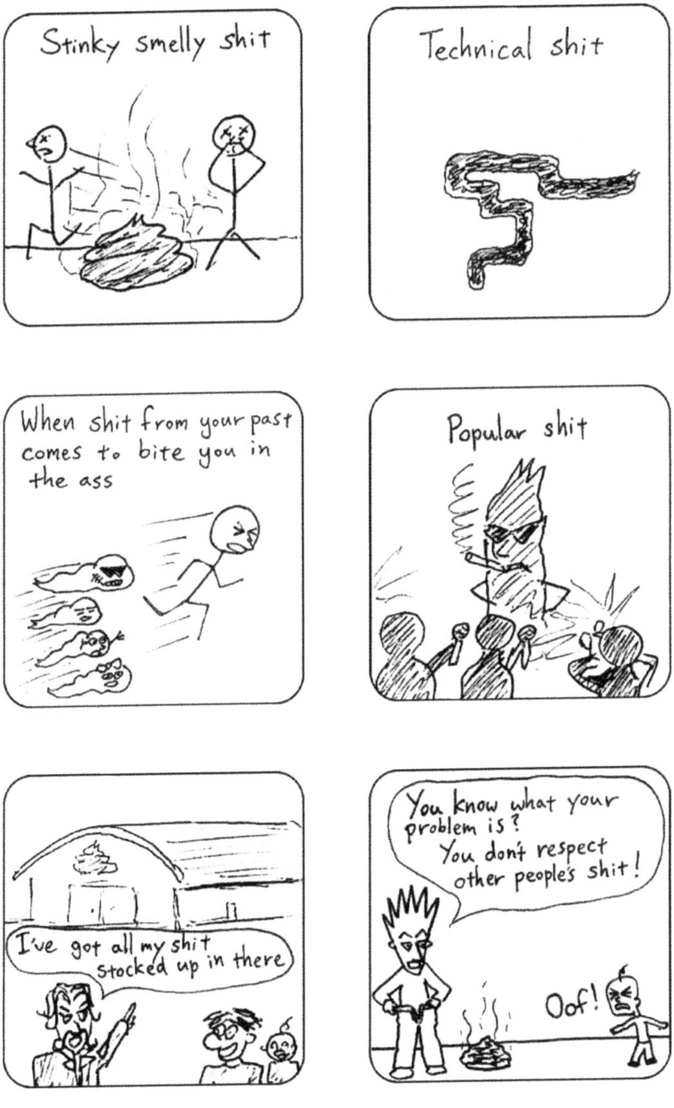
Stinky smelly shit
Technical shit
When shit from your past comes to bite you in the ass
Popular shit
I've got all my shit stocked up in there
You know what your problem is? You don't respect other people's shit!
Oof!

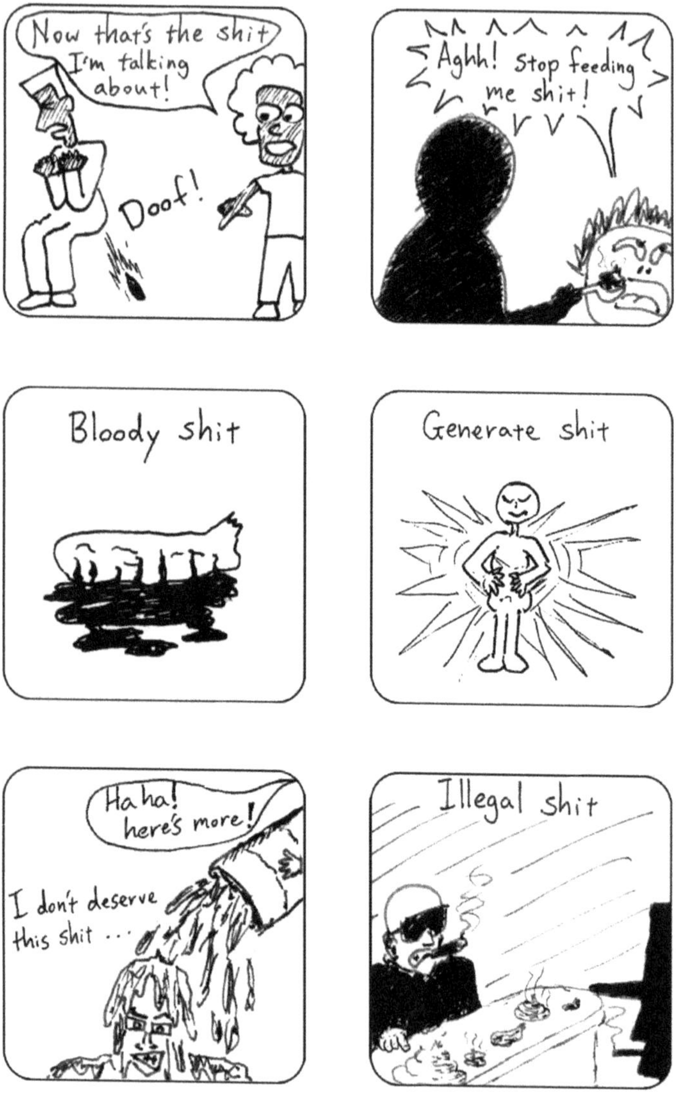
Now that's the shit I'm talking about!
Doof!
Aghh! Stop feeding me shit!
Bloody shit
Generate shit
Haha! here's more!
I don't deserve this shit ...
Illegal shit

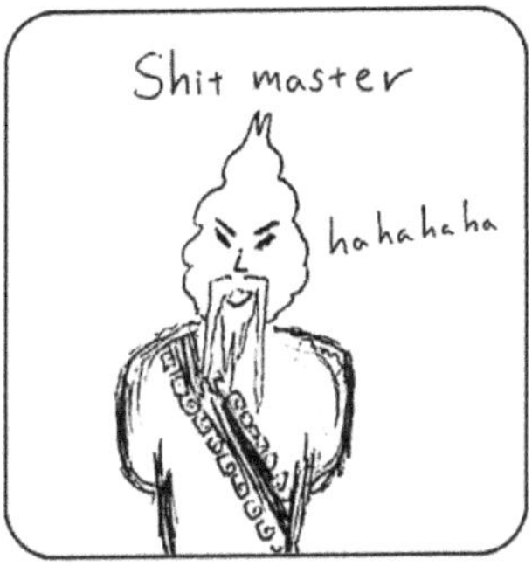
Shit master
hahahaha

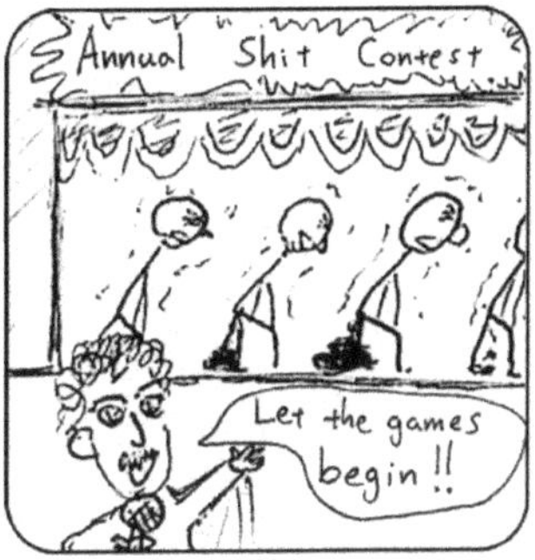
Annual Shit Contest
Let the games begin!!

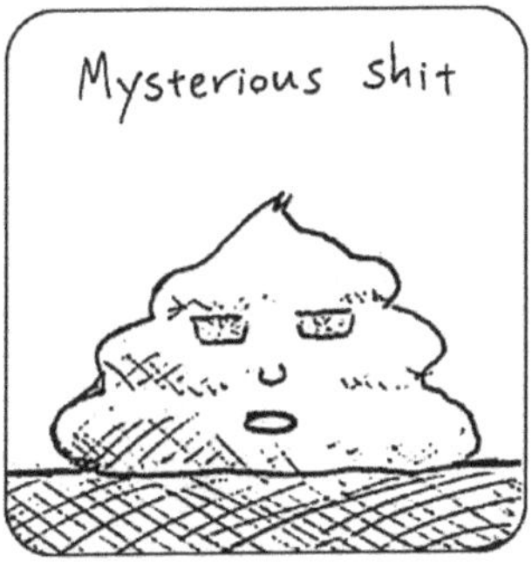
Mysterious shit

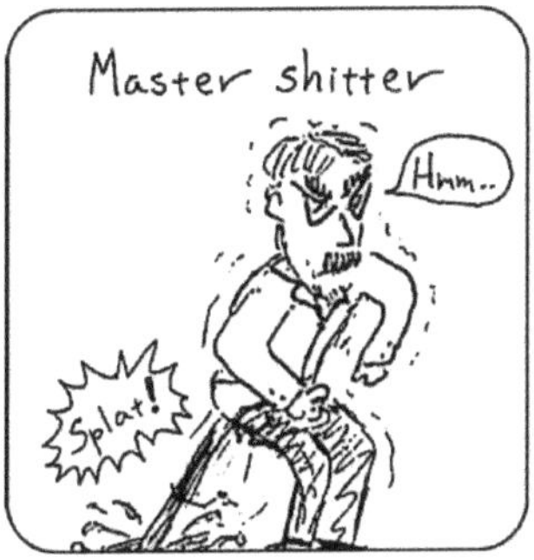
Master shitter
Hmm..
Splat!

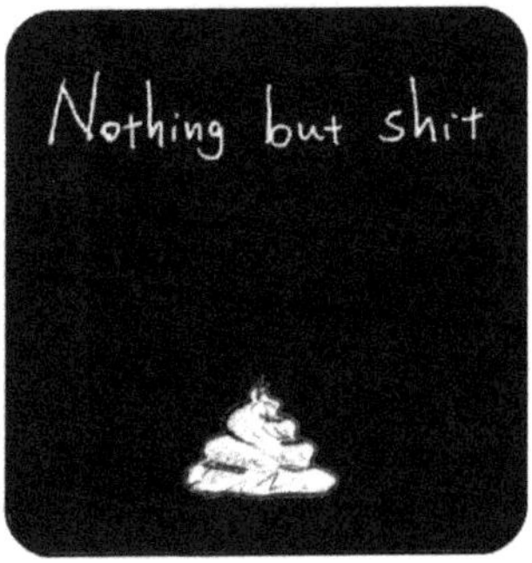
Nothing but shit

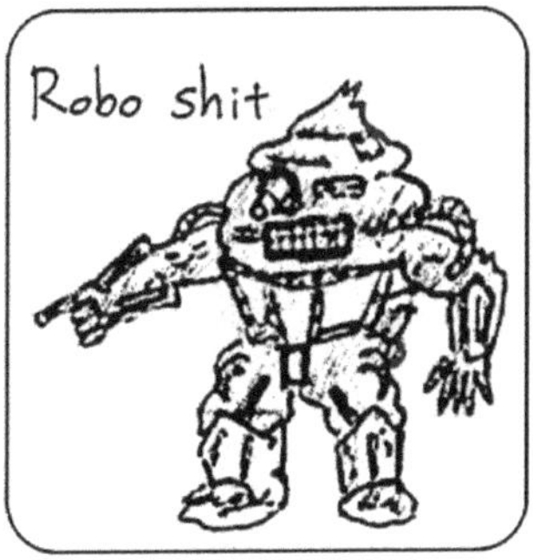
Robo shit

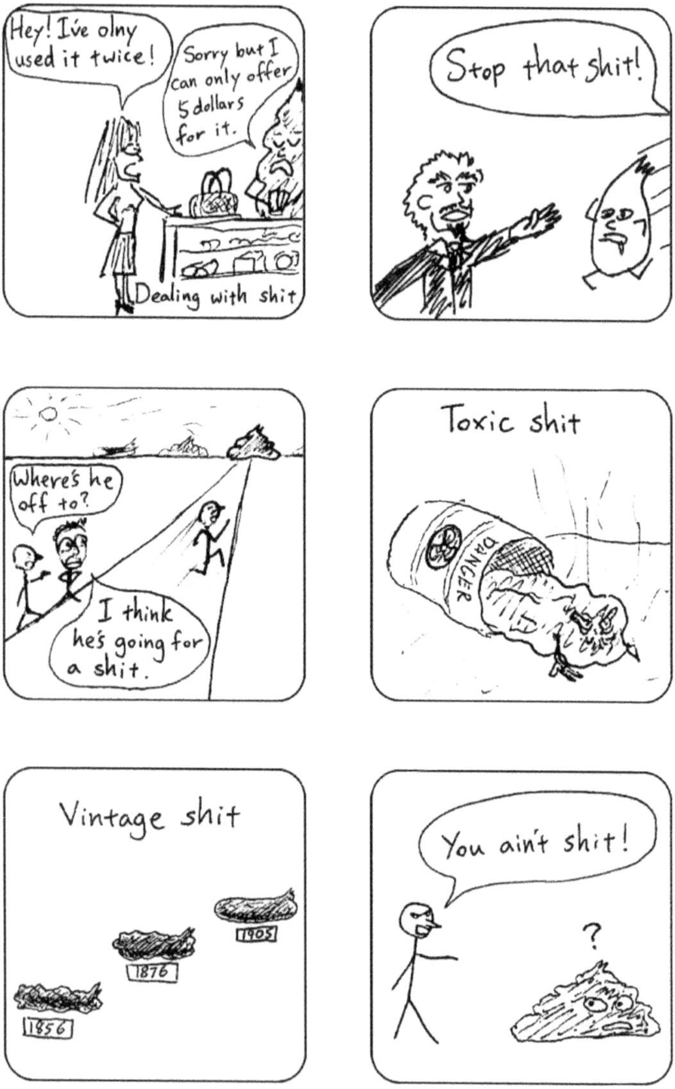
Hey! I've olny used it twice!
Sorry but I can only offer 5 dollars for it.
Dealing with shit
Stop that shit!
Where's he off to?
I think he's going for a shit.
Toxic shit
DANGER
Vintage shit
1905
1876
1856
You ain't shit!
?

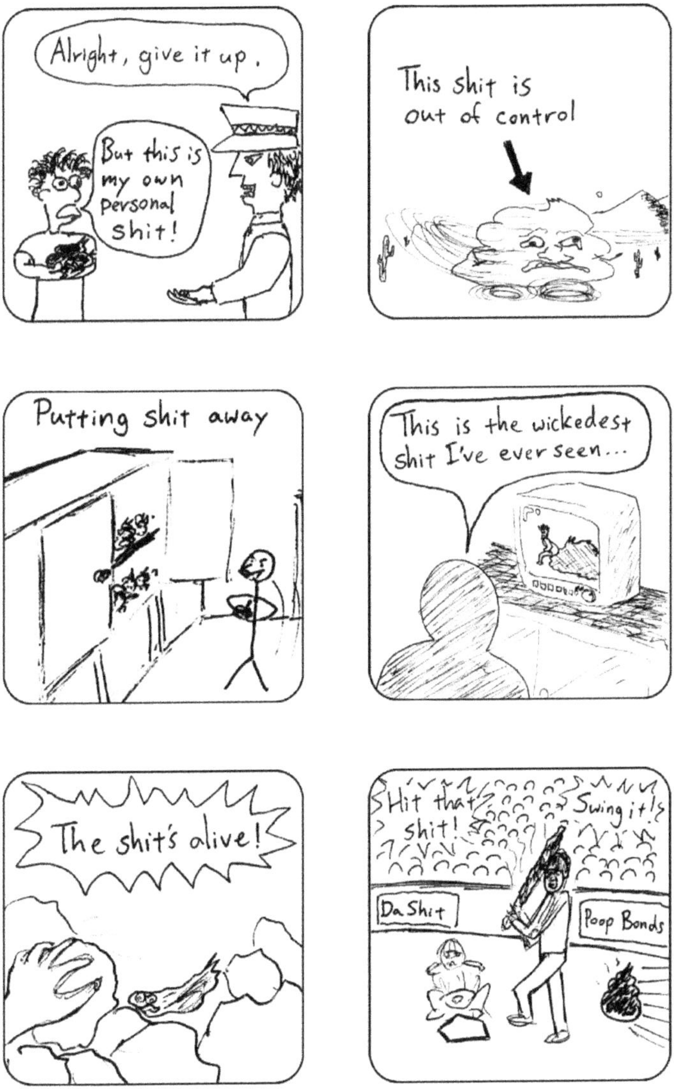
Alright, give it up.
But this is my own personal shit!
This shit is out of control
Putting shit away
This is the wickedest shit I've ever seen...
The shit's alive!
Hit that shit!
Swing it!
Da Shit
Poop Bonds

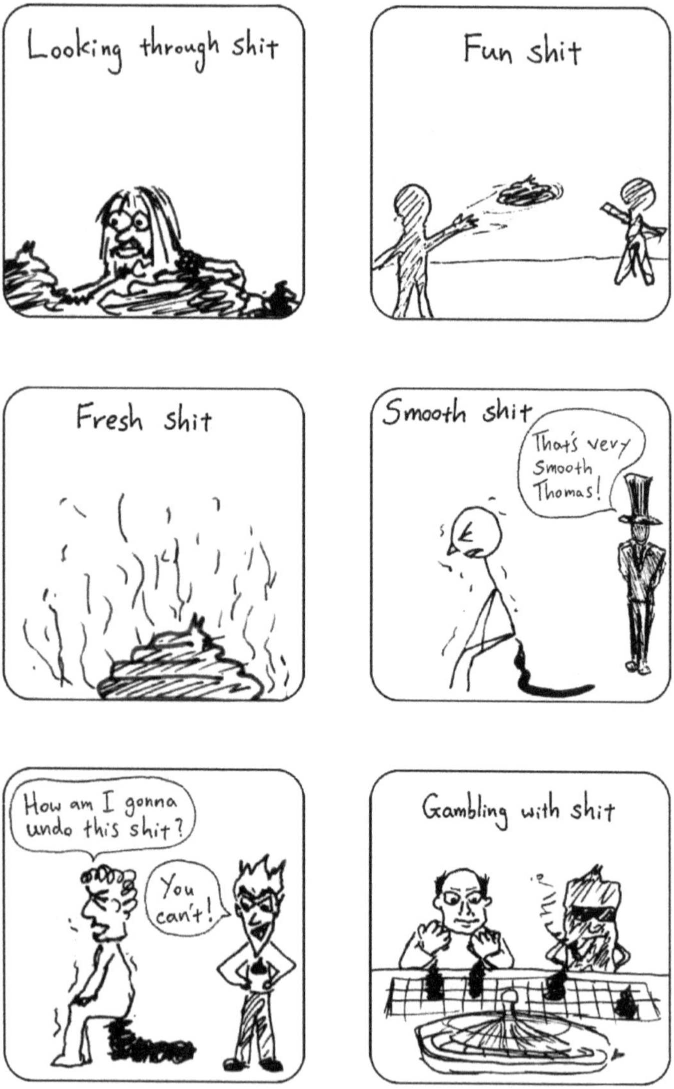
Looking through shit
Fun shit
Fresh shit
Smooth shit
That's very Smooth Thomas!
How am I gonna undo this shit?
You can't!
Gambling with shit

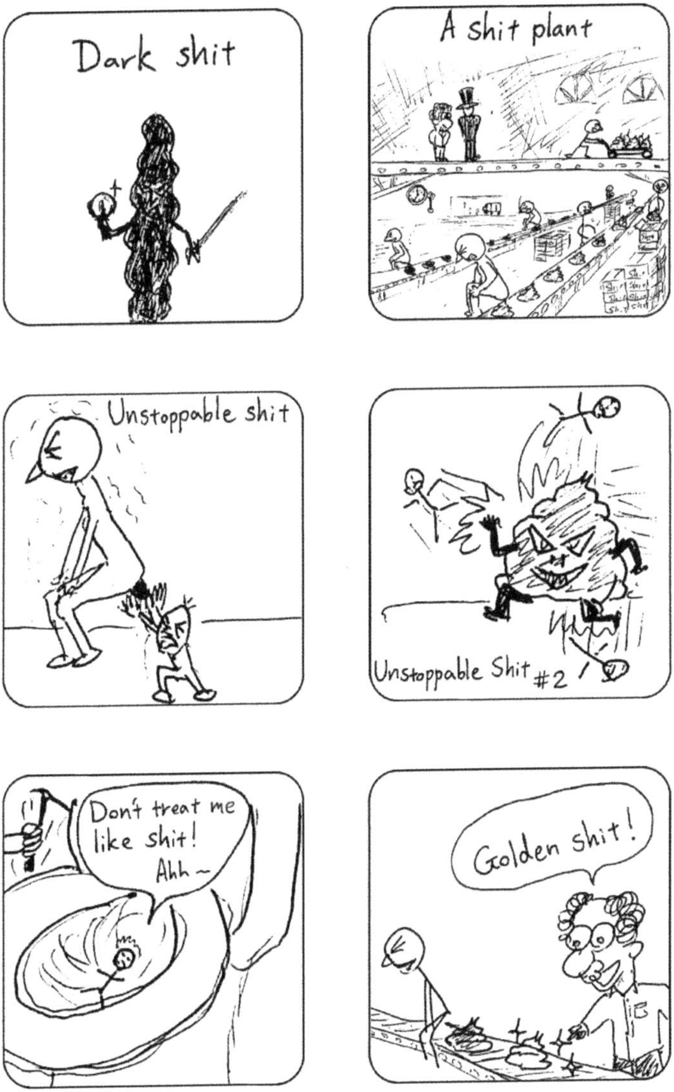
Dark shit
A shit plant
Unstoppable shit
Unstoppable Shit #2
Don't treat me like shit! Ahh~
Golden shit!

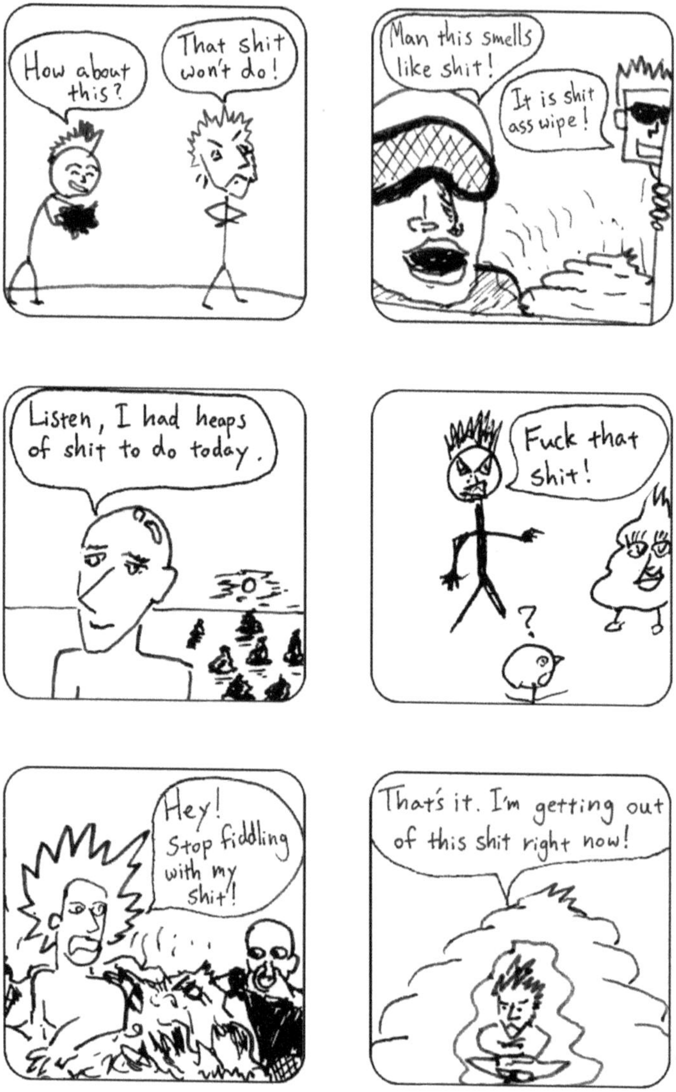
How about this?
That shit won't do!
Man this smells like shit!
It is shit ass wipe!
Listen, I had heaps of shit to do today.
Fuck that shit!
?
Hey! Stop fiddling with my shit!
That's it. I'm getting out of this shit right now!

What did you say? You little shit!
But...

The shit popped out
Pop!

Shitland

Shitland sheepdog

The Shit Show!!

Frozen shit

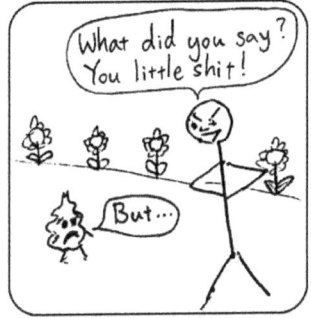

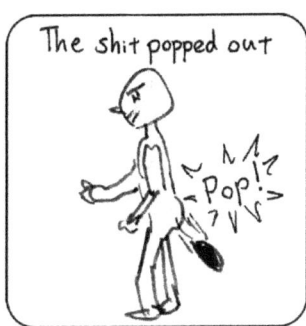

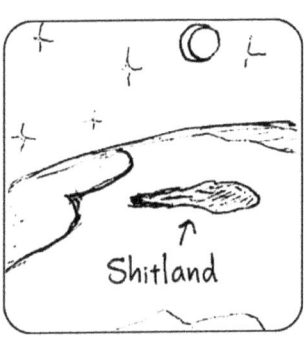

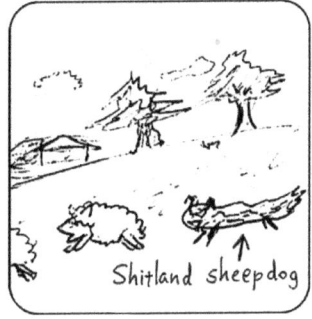

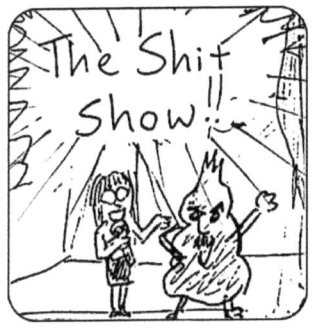

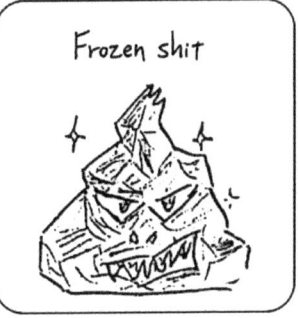

Shit cycle

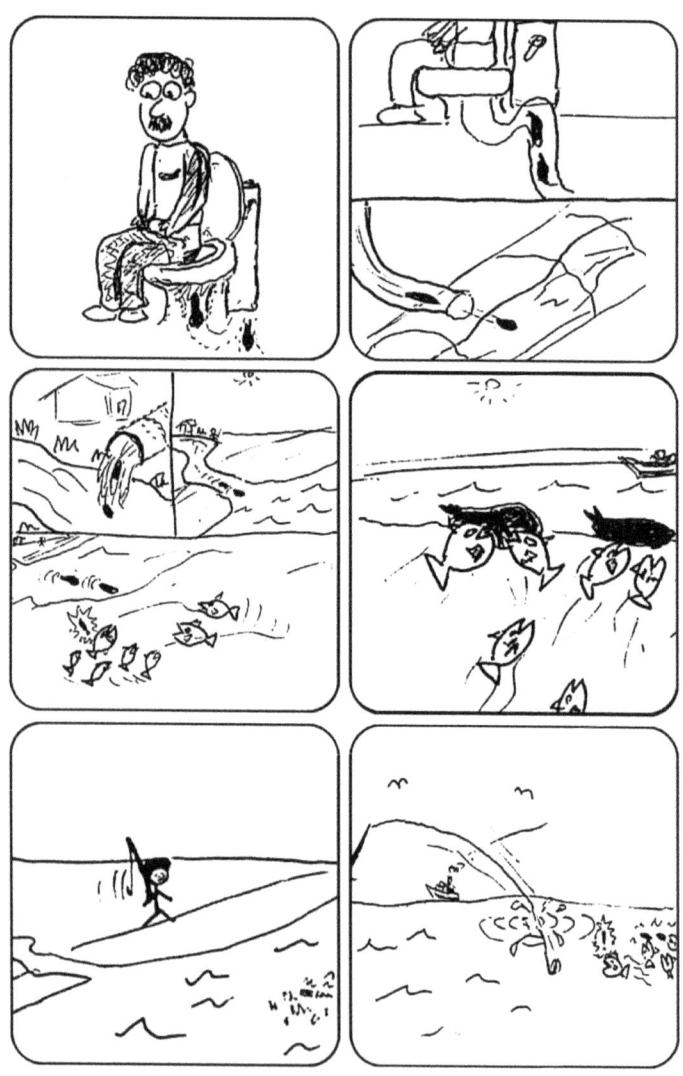

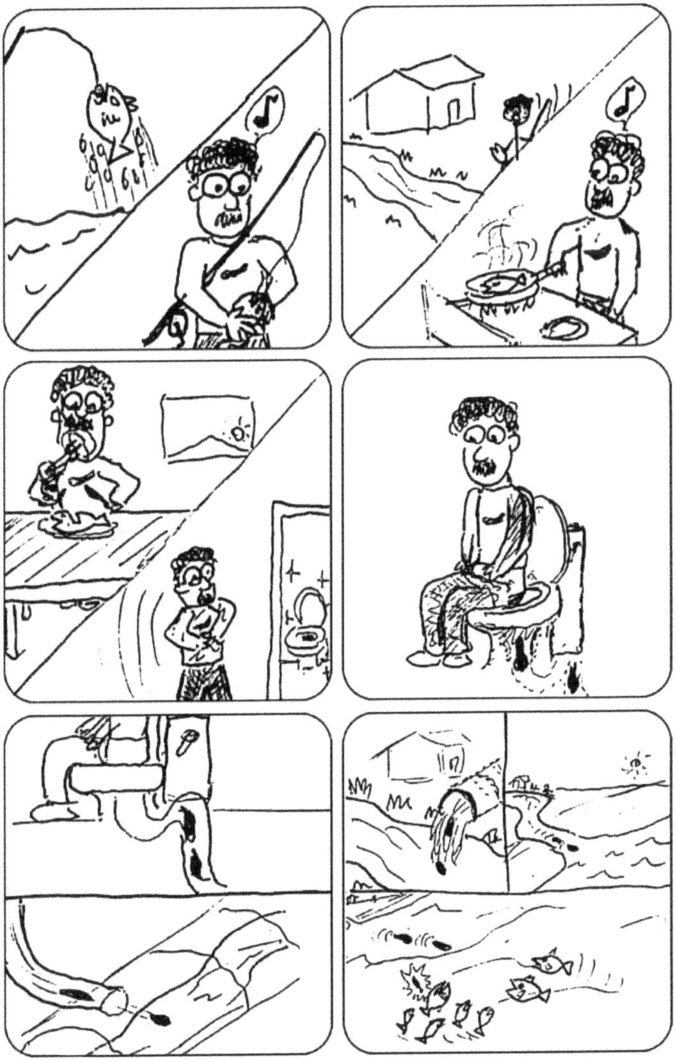

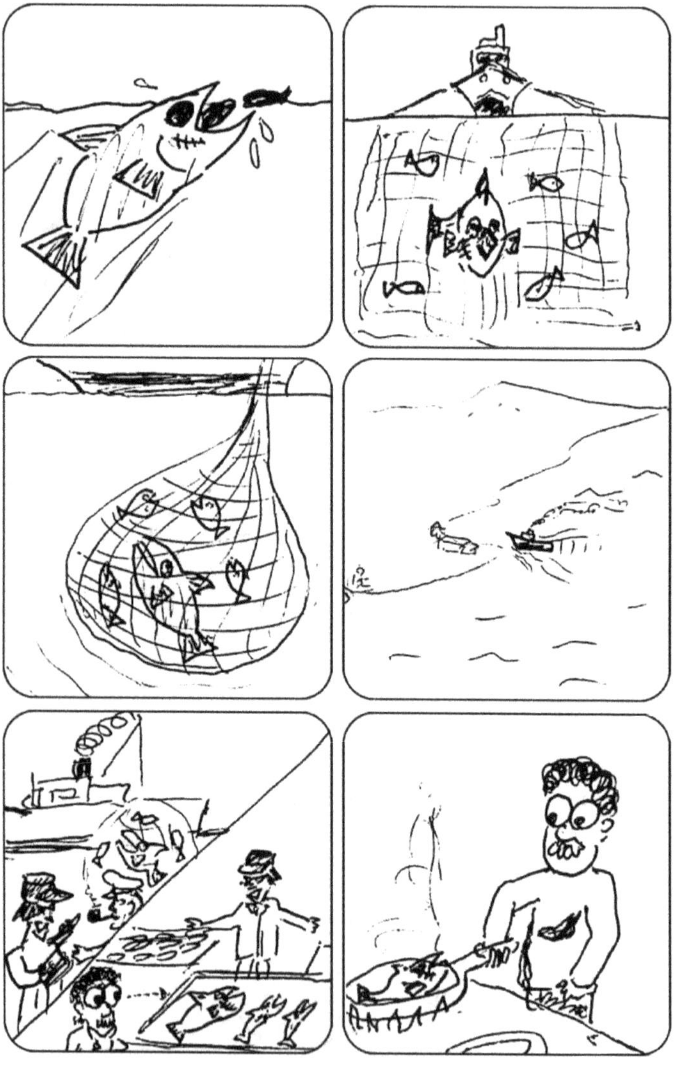

4

More shit

I'm proud to introduce our first genetically modified shit.
Planting shit
Watering shit
I've been chasing that shit for so long...

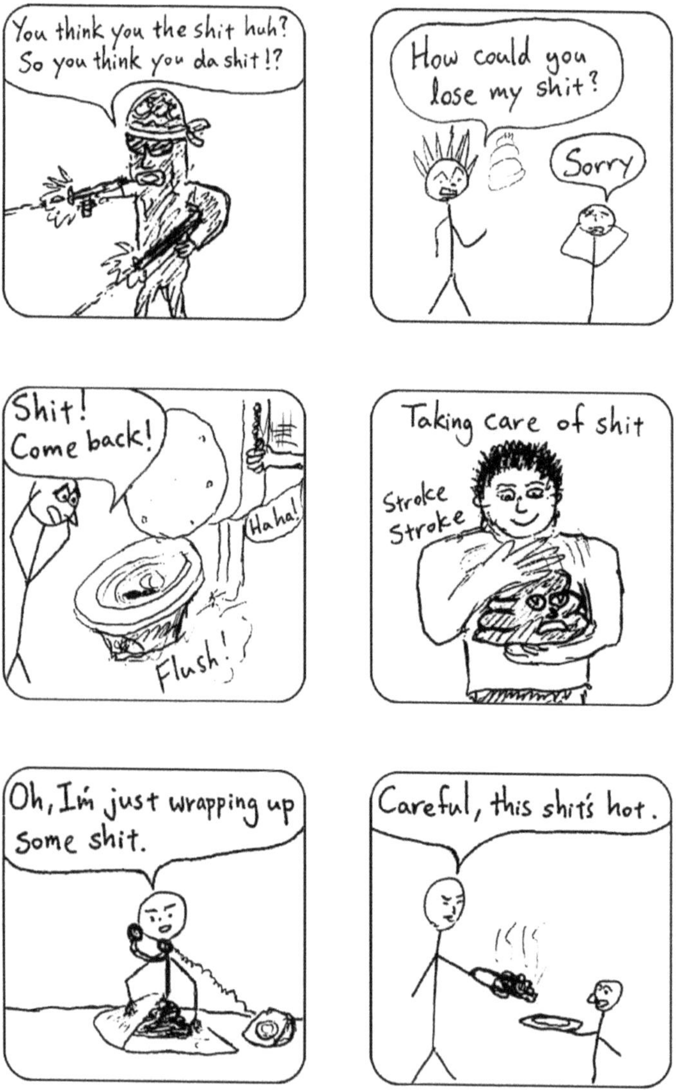
You think you the shit huh? So you think you da shit!?
How could you lose my shit?
Sorry
Shit! Come back!
Haha!
Flush!
Taking care of shit
Stroke Stroke
Oh, I'm just wrapping up some shit.
Careful, this shit's hot.

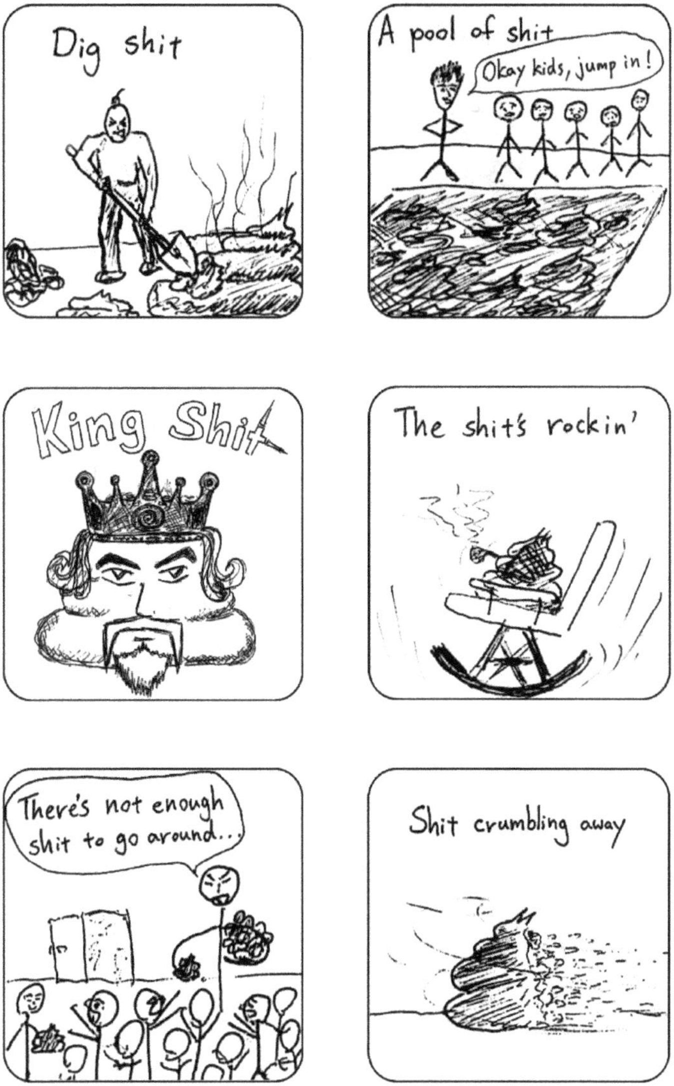
Dig shit
A pool of shit
Okay kids, jump in!
King Shit
The shit's rockin'
There's not enough shit to go around...
Shit crumbling away

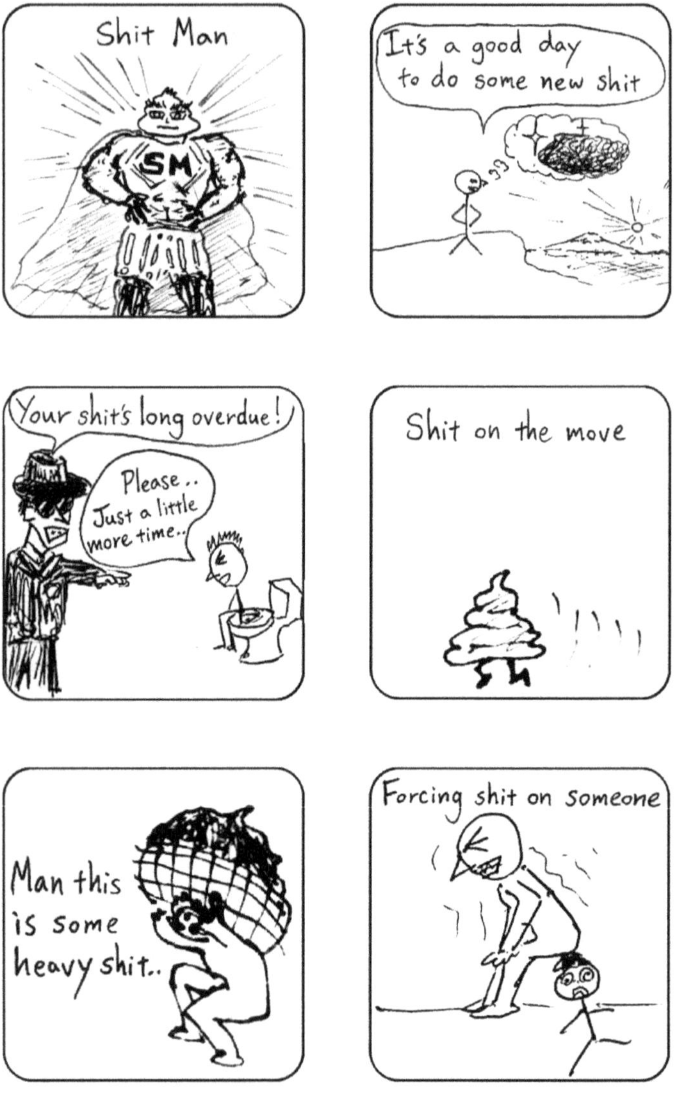
Shit Man
SM
It's a good day to do some new shit
Your shit's long overdue!
Please.. Just a little more time..
Shit on the move
Man this is some heavy shit..
Forcing shit on someone

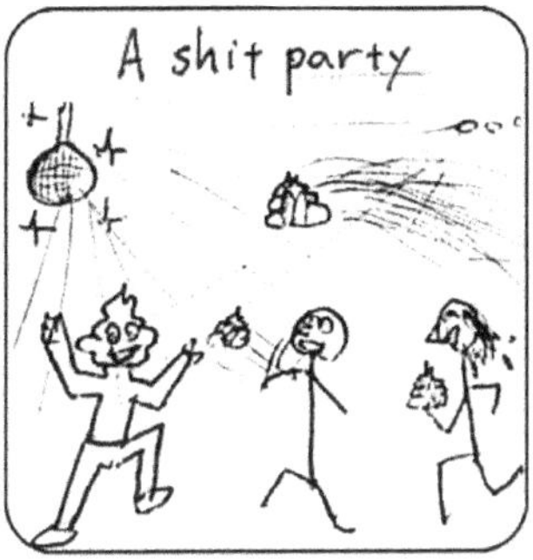
A shit party

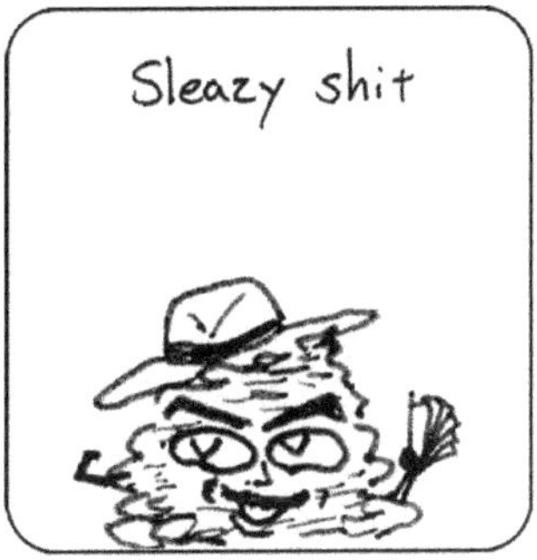
Sleazy shit

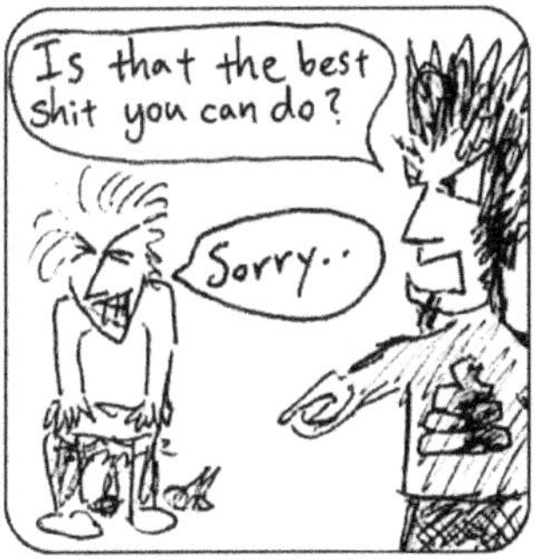
Is that the best shit you can do?
Sorry..

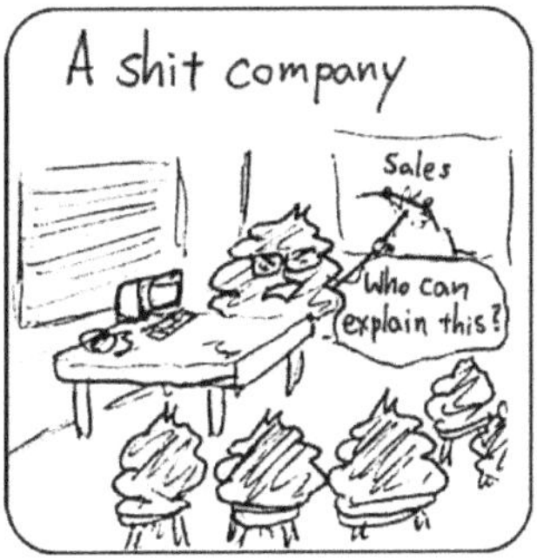
A shit company
Sales
Who can explain this?

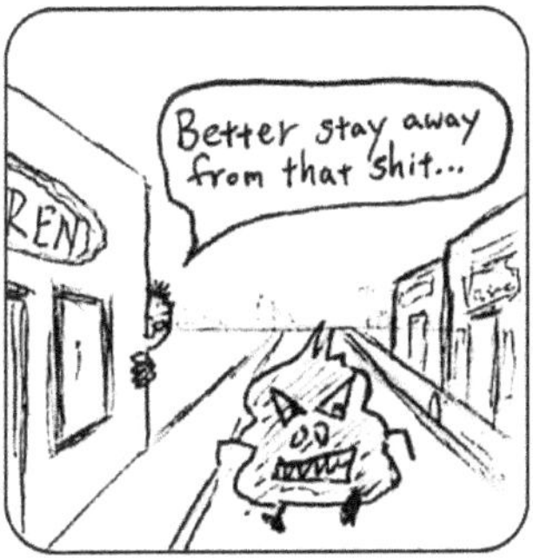
Better stay away from that shit...

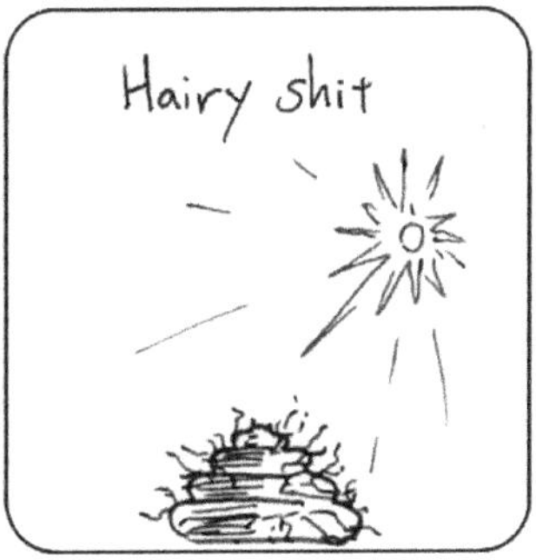
Hairy shit

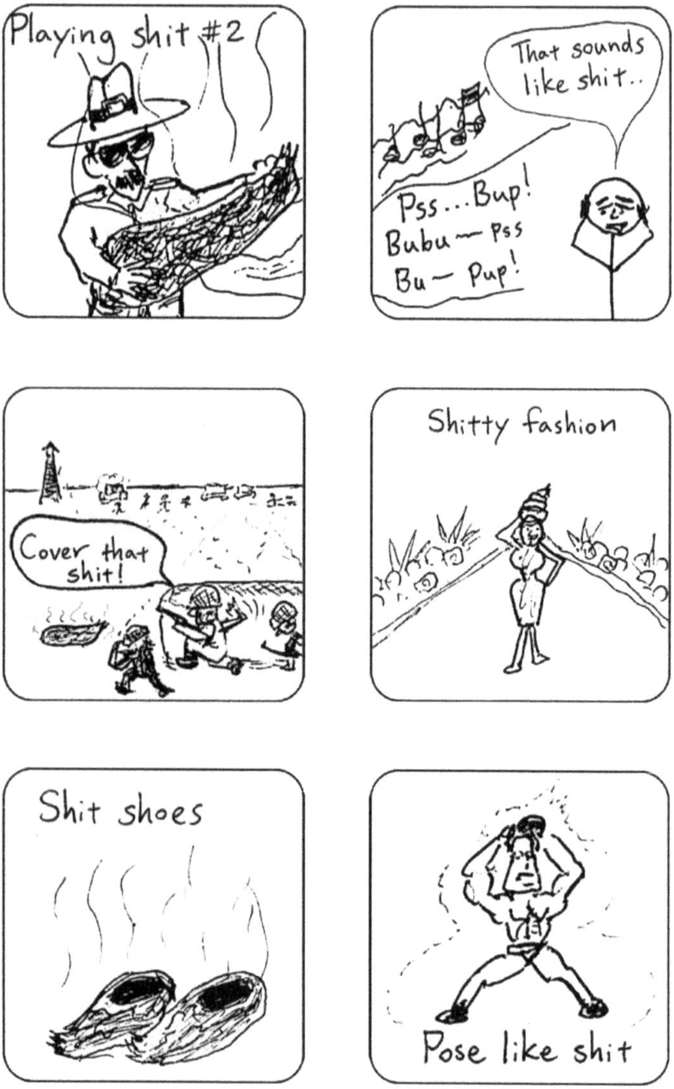
Playing shit #2
That sounds like shit..
Pss...Bup!
Bubu~ Pss
Bu~ Pup!
Cover that shit!
Shitty fashion
Shit shoes
Pose like shit

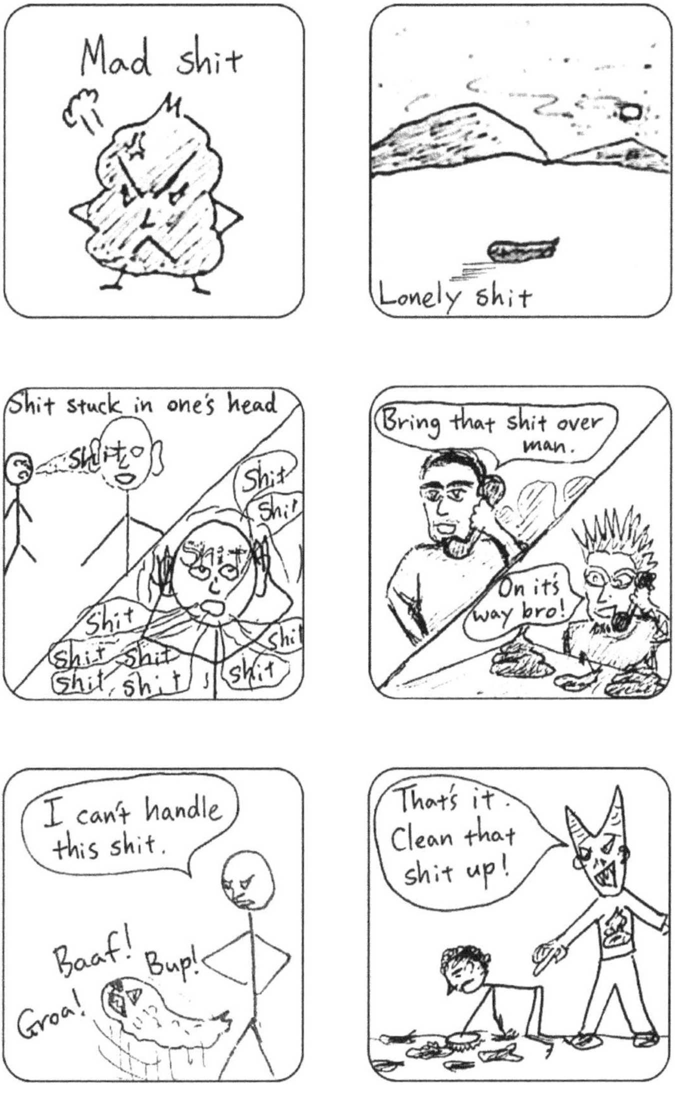
Mad shit
Lonely shit
Shit stuck in one's head
Shit
Shit
Shit
Shit
Shit
Shit
Shit
Bring that shit over man.
On it's way bro!
I can't handle this shit.
Baaf!
Bup!
Groa!
That's it. Clean that shit up!

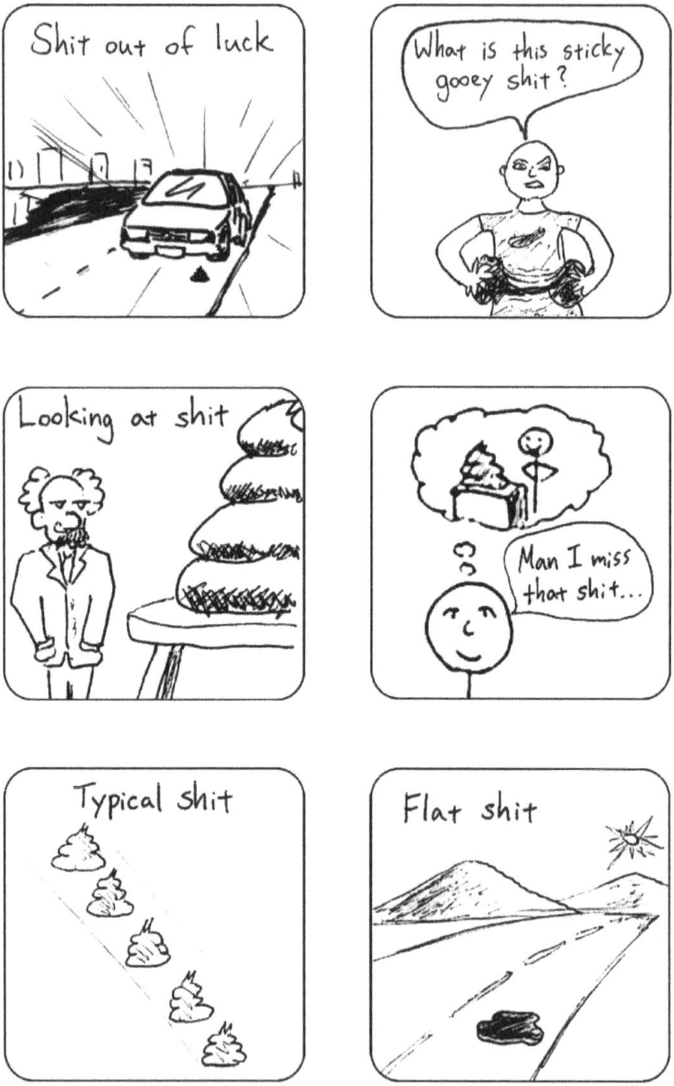
Shit out of luck
What is this sticky gooey shit?
Looking at shit
Man I miss that shit...
Typical shit
Flat shit

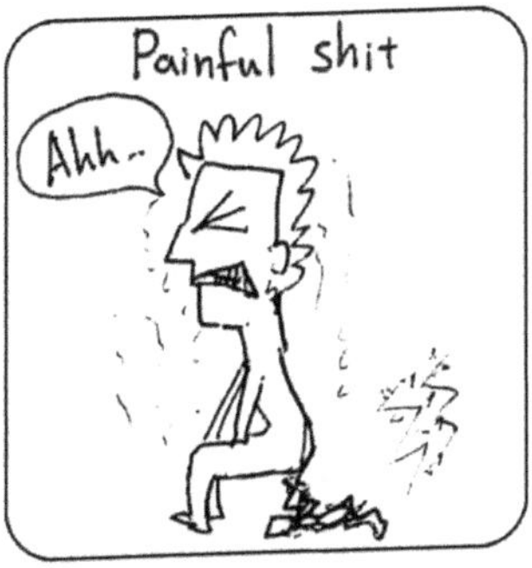
Painful shit
Ahh..

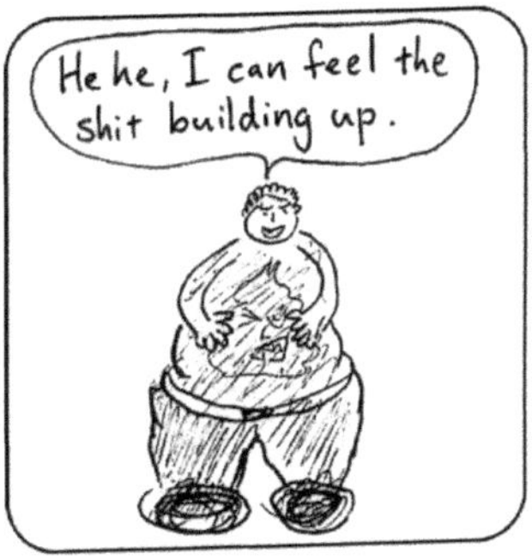
He he, I can feel the shit building up.

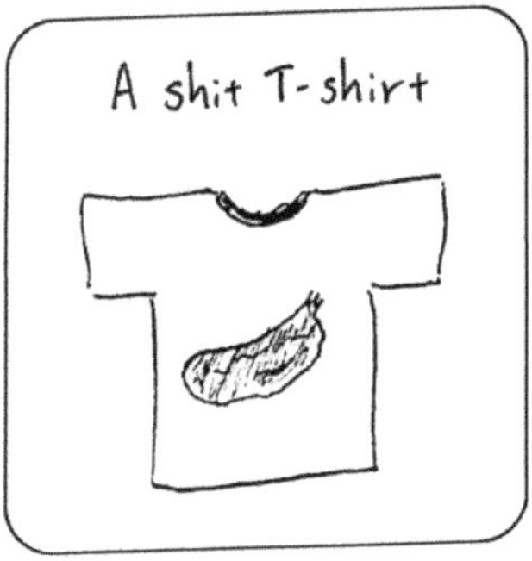
A shit T-shirt

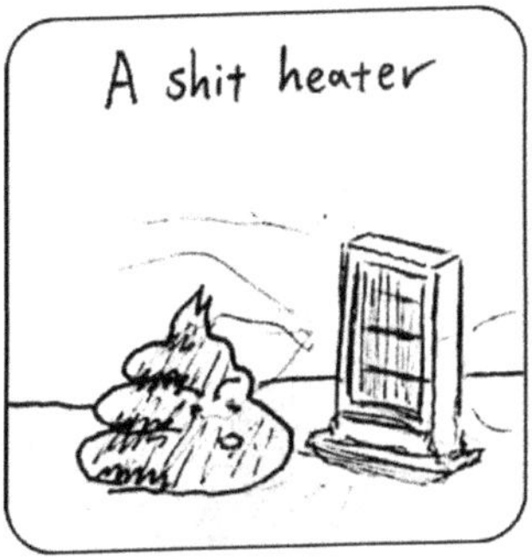
A shit heater

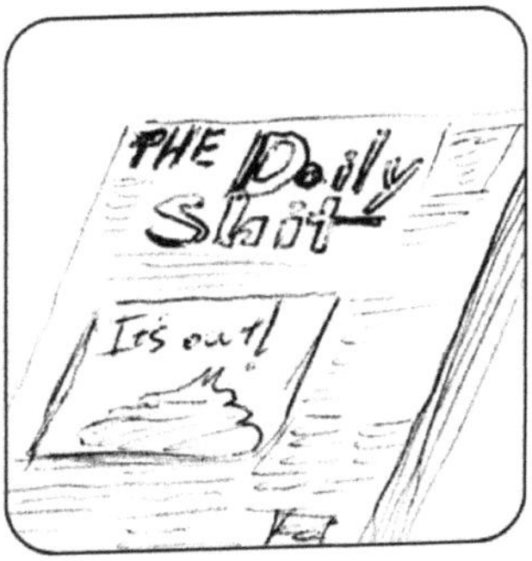
THE Daily Shit
It's out!

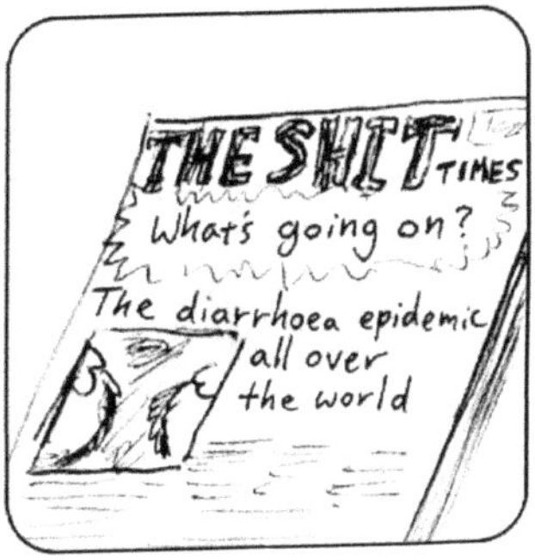
THE SHIT TIMES
What's going on?
The diarrhoea epidemic all over the world

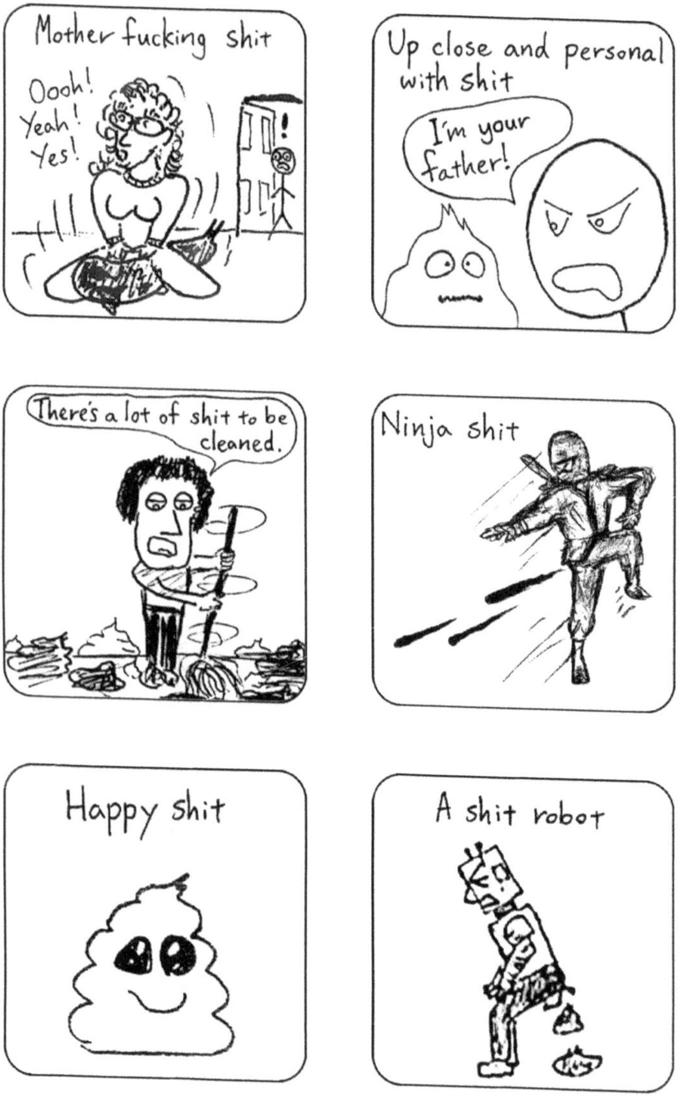
Mother fucking shit
Oooh! Yeah! Yes!
!
Up close and personal with shit
I'm your father!
There's a lot of shit to be cleaned.
Ninja shit
Happy shit
A shit robot

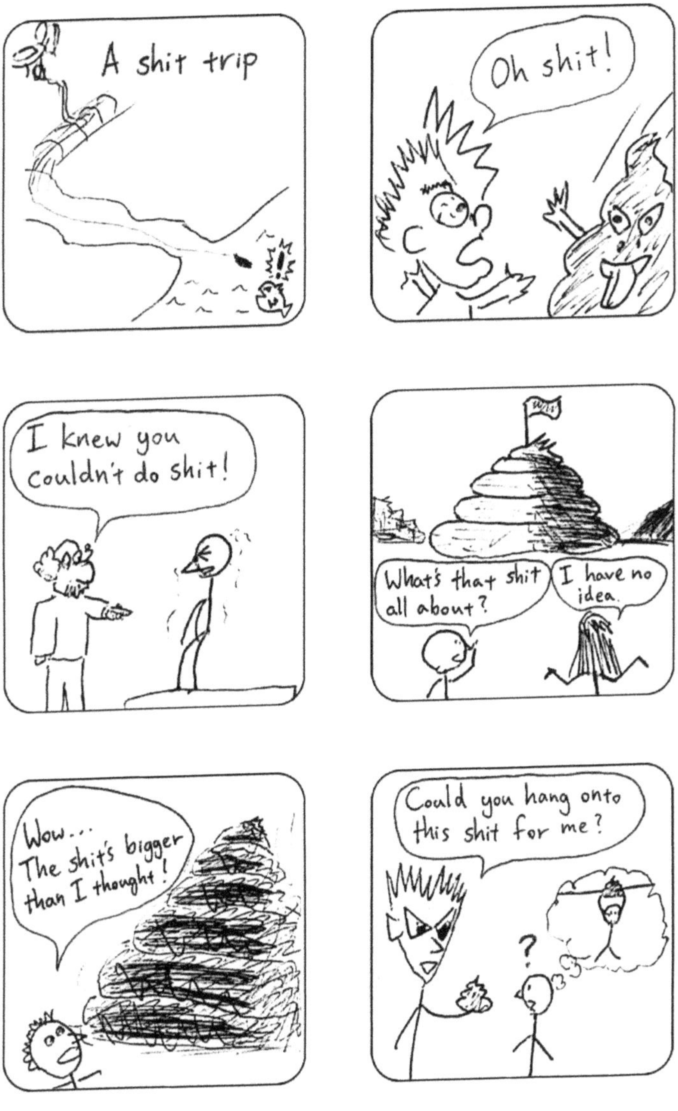
A shit trip
Oh shit!
I knew you couldn't do shit!
What's that shit all about?
I have no idea.
Wow...
The shit's bigger than I thought!
Could you hang onto this shit for me?

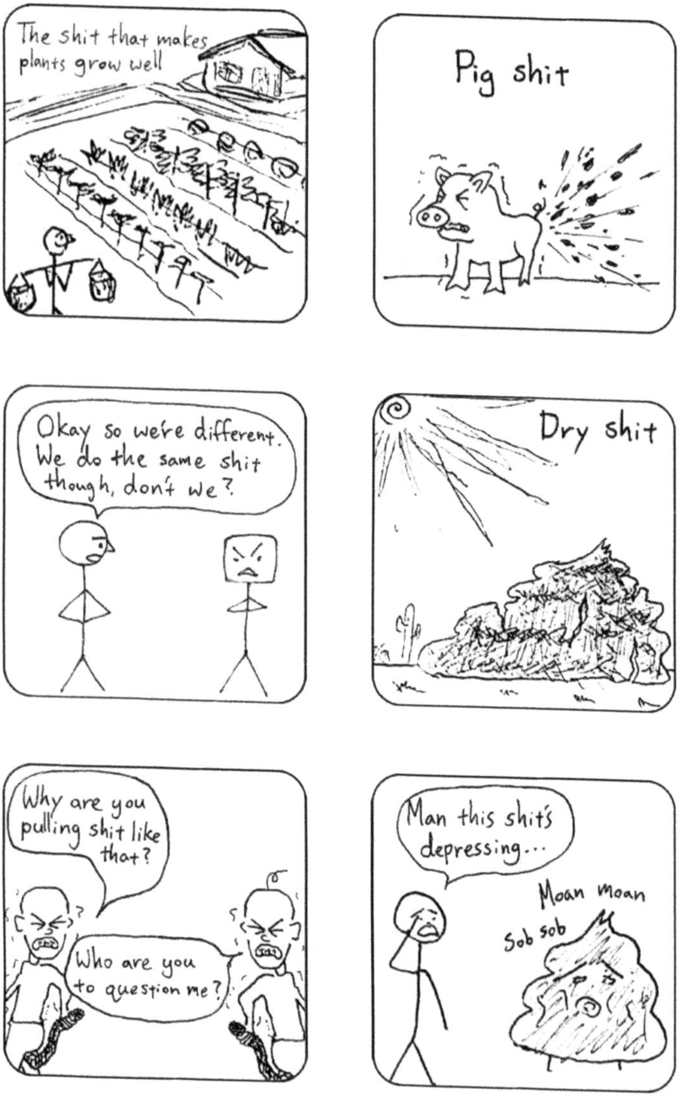
The shit that makes plants grow well
Pig shit
Okay so we're different. We do the same shit though, don't we?
Dry shit
Why are you pulling shit like that?
Who are you to question me?
Man this shit's depressing...
Moan moan
Sob sob

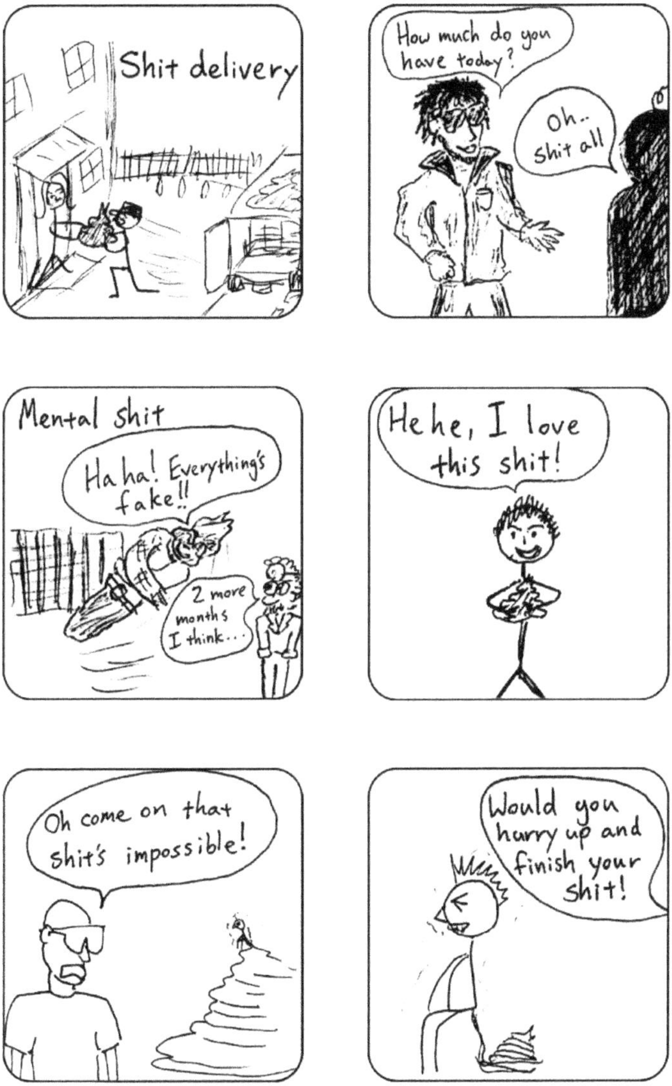
Shit delivery
How much do you have today?
Oh.. shit all
Mental shit
Ha ha! Everything's fake!!
2 more months I think...
He he, I love this shit!
Oh come on that shit's impossible!
Would you hurry up and finish your shit!

Shit of the Undead
Dr. Frank has been studying the undead.. What did he discover?
Hmm.. there must be a way to figure this shit out. I need another specimen...
Why do we have to do the same old shit everyday huh?
Yeah, the same fuckin' shit!
Here dock a new... Hey! Aaaaa! Aaagh!
Oh shit!
It's too late.. let it finish. This is what I need for the next step.
Munch! Munch!
Next, we'll chain the zombie to that box over there... and see what happens.

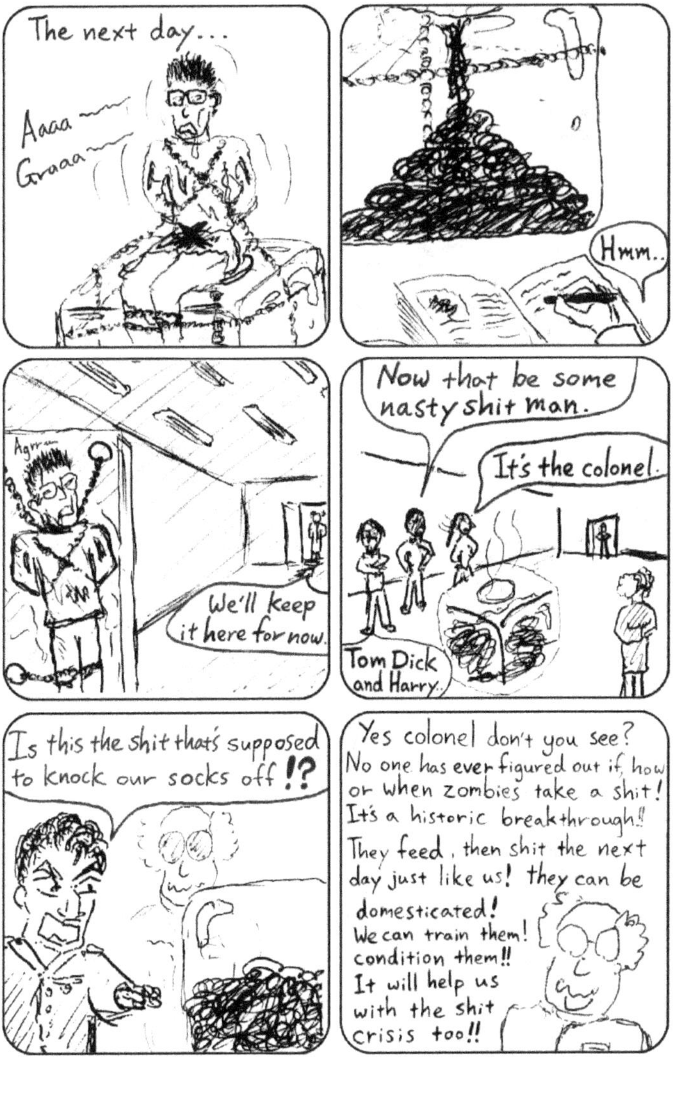
The next day...
Aaaa Graaa
Hmm..
Agrr
We'll keep it here for now.
Now that be some nasty shit man.
It's the colonel.
Tom Dick and Harry.
Is this the shit that's supposed to knock our socks off !?
Yes colonel don't you see? No one has ever figured out if, how or when zombies take a shit! It's a historic breakthrough!! They feed, then shit the next day just like us! they can be domesticated! We can train them! condition them!! It will help us with the shit crisis too!!

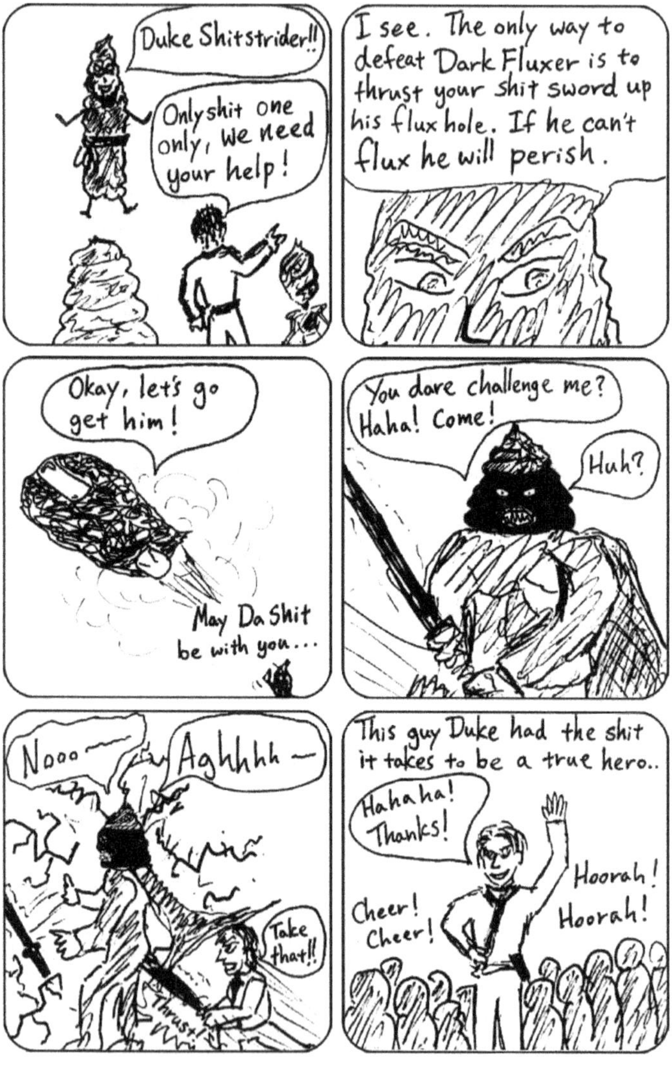
Duke Shitstrider!!
Onlyshit one only, we need your help!
I see. The only way to defeat Dark Fluxer is to thrust your shit sword up his flux hole. If he can't flux he will perish.
Okay, let's go get him!
May Da Shit be with you...
You dare challenge me? Haha! Come!
Huh?
Nooo~
Aghhhh~
Take that!!
Thrust!
This guy Duke had the shit it takes to be a true hero..
Hahaha! Thanks!
Cheer! Cheer!
Hoorah! Hoorah!

5

Going beyond

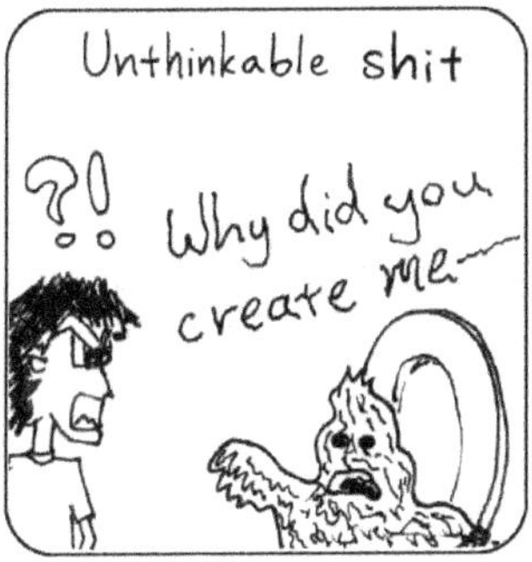
Unthinkable shit
?!
Why did you create me

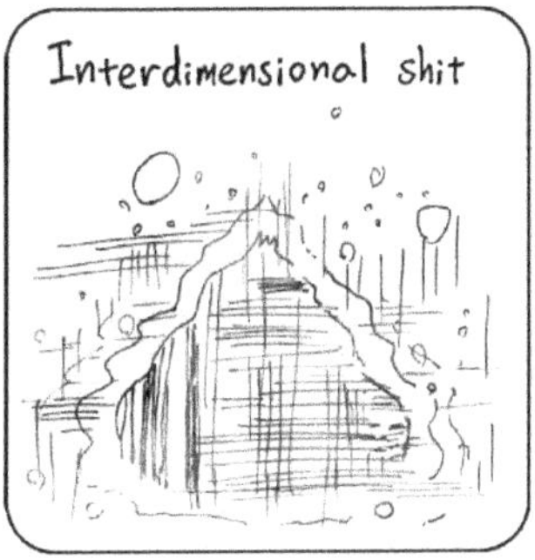
Interdimensional shit

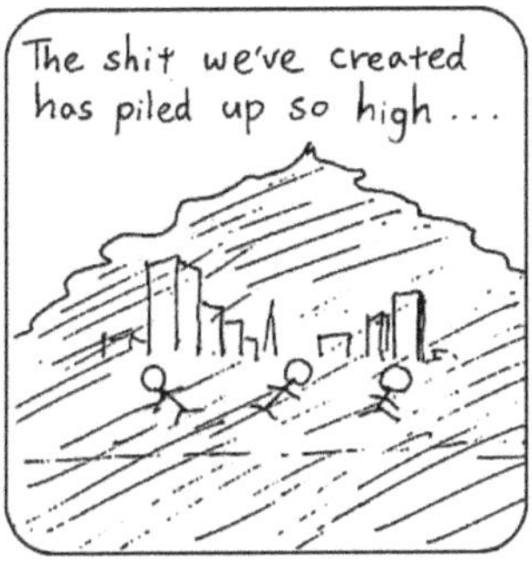
The shit we've created has piled up so high . . .

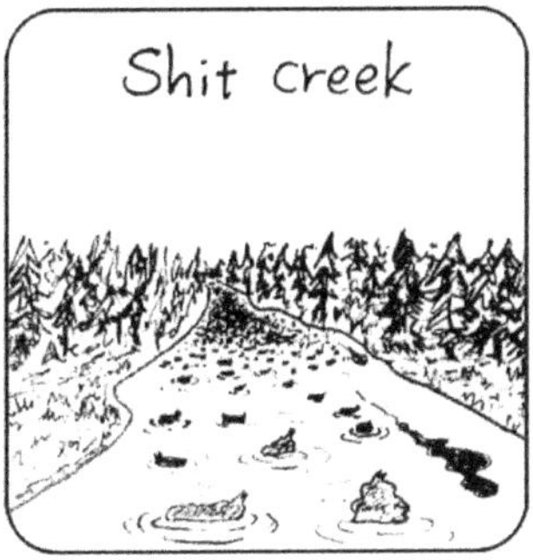
Shit creek

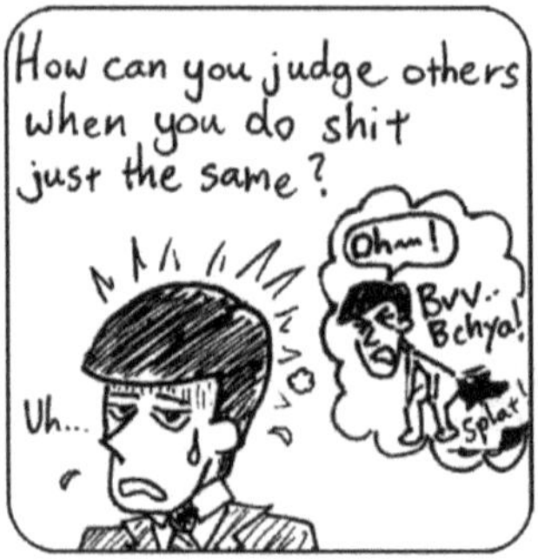
How can you judge others when you do shit just the same?
Uh...
Oh~!
Bvv.. Bchya!
Splat!

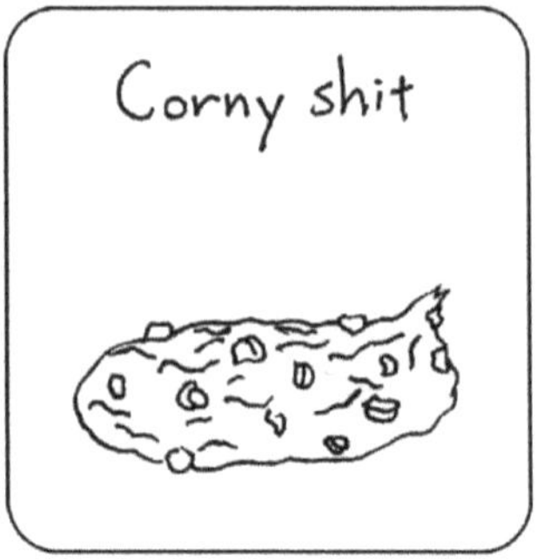
Corny shit

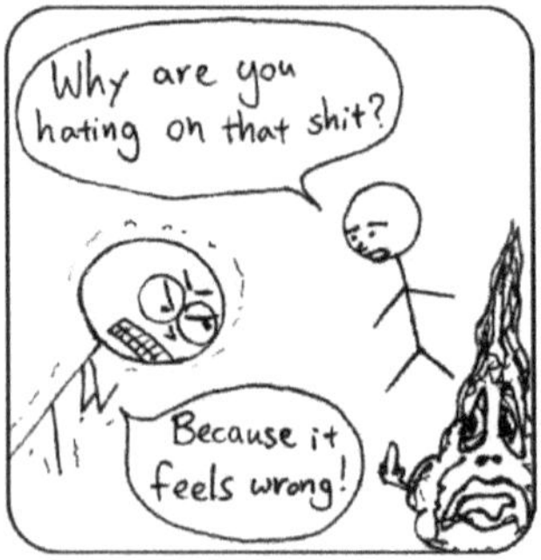
Why are you hating on that shit?
Because it feels wrong!

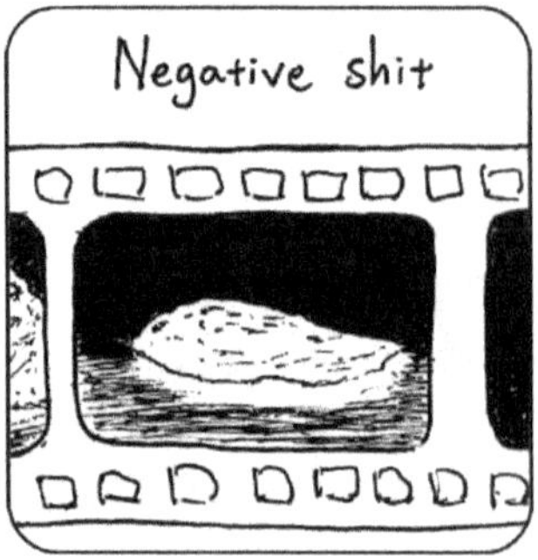
Negative shit

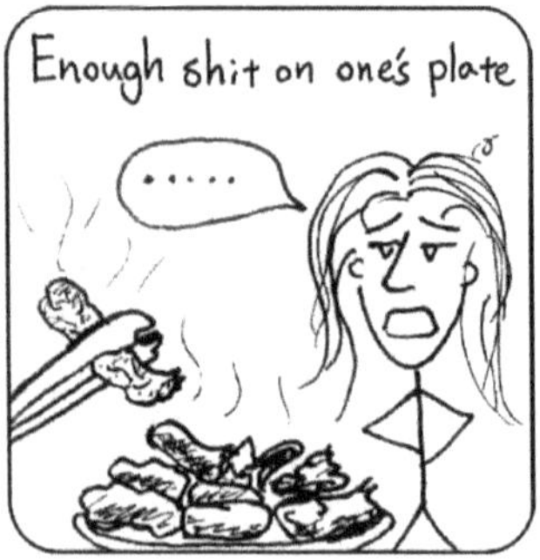
Enough shit on one's plate
.....

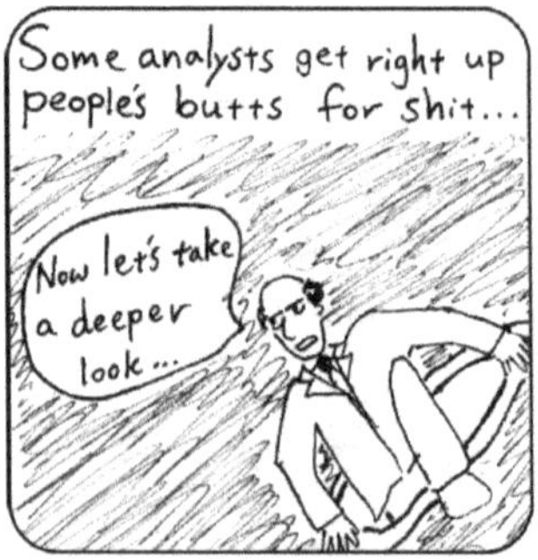
Some analysts get right up people's butts for shit...
Now let's take a deeper look...

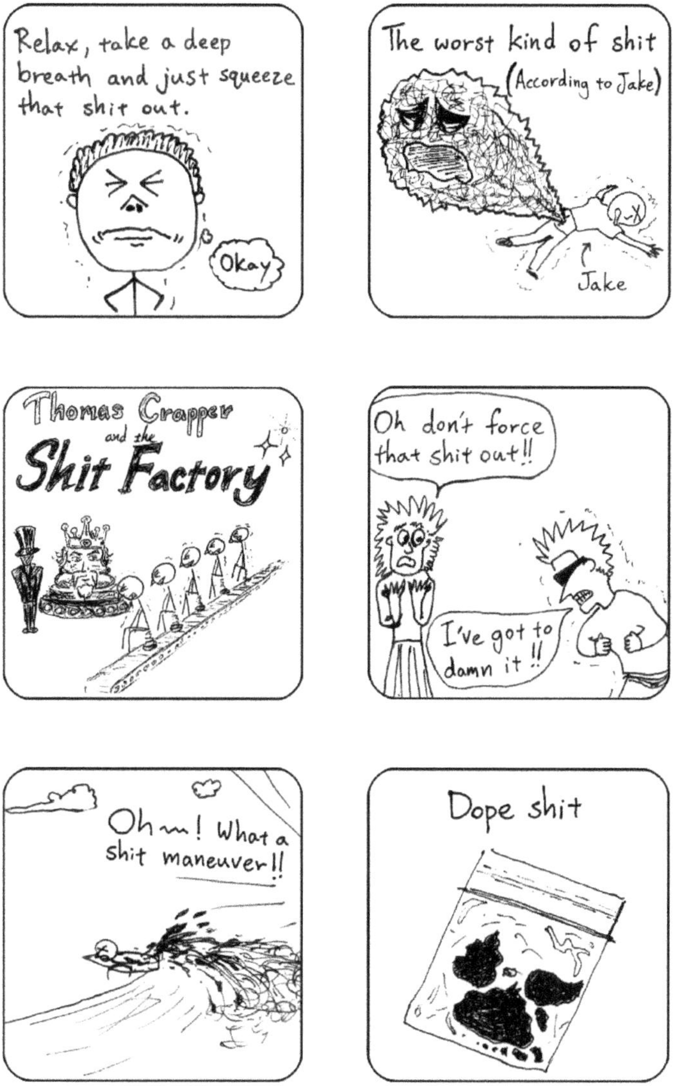
Relax, take a deep breath and just squeeze that shit out.
Okay
The worst kind of shit
(According to Jake)
Jake
Thomas Crapper and the Shit Factory
Oh don't force that shit out!!
I've got to damn it!!
Oh~! What a shit maneuver!!
Dope shit

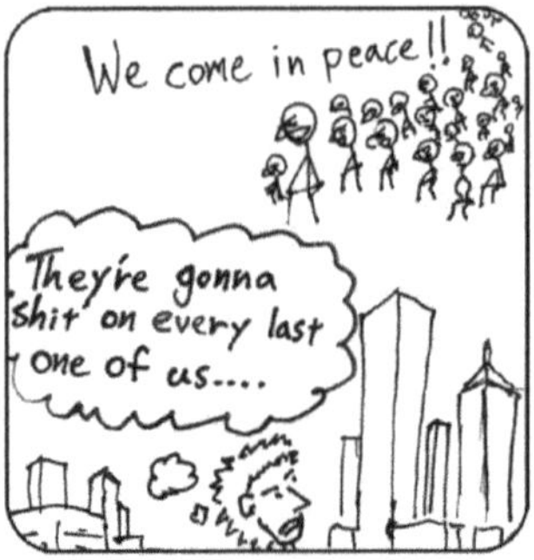
We come in peace!!
They're gonna shit on every last one of us....

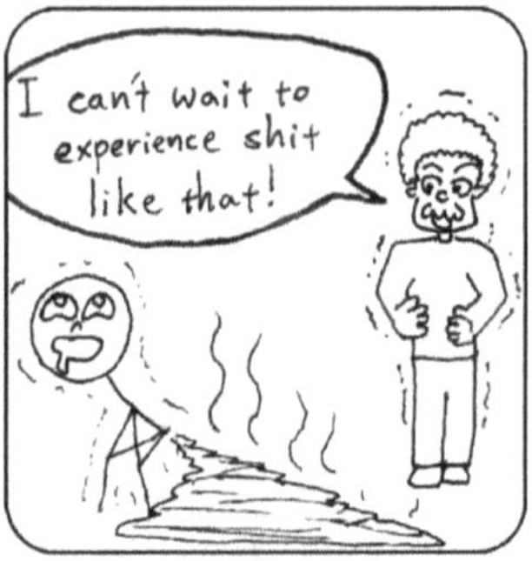
I can't wait to experience shit like that!

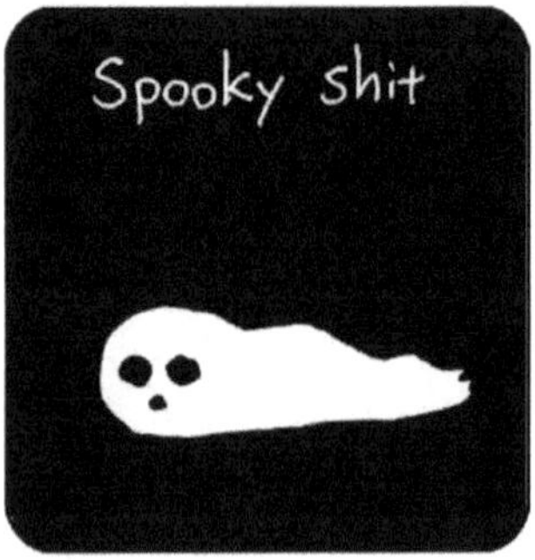
Spooky shit

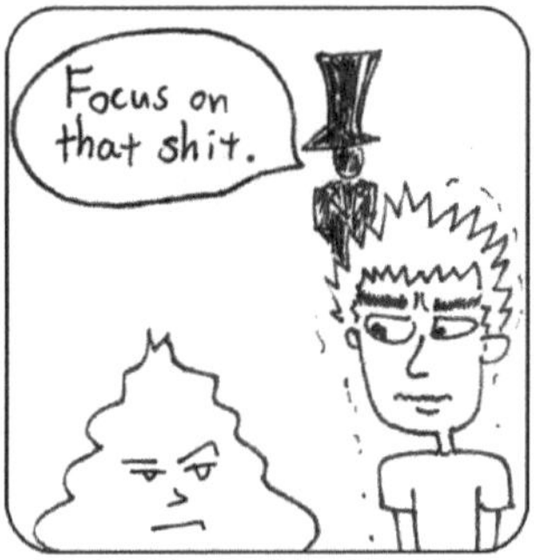
Focus on that shit.

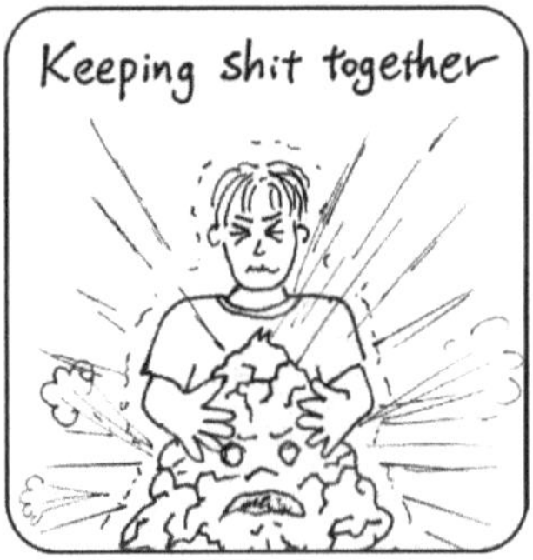
Keeping shit together

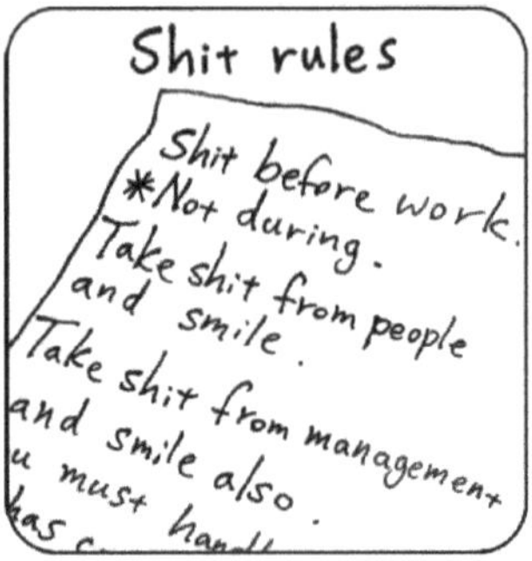
Shit rules
Shit before work.
*Not during.
Take shit from people and smile.
Take shit from management and smile also.

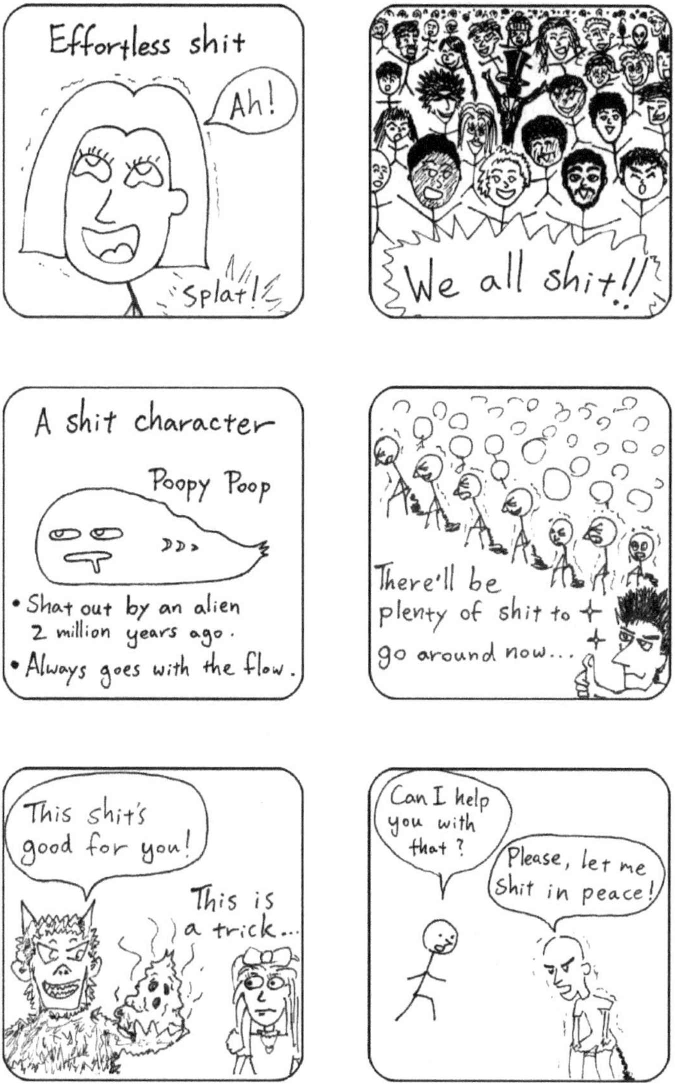
Effortless shit
Ah!
Splat!
We all shit!!
A shit character
Poopy Poop
• Shat out by an alien 2 million years ago.
• Always goes with the flow.
There'll be plenty of shit to go around now...
This shit's good for you!
This is a trick...
Can I help you with that?
Please, let me shit in peace!

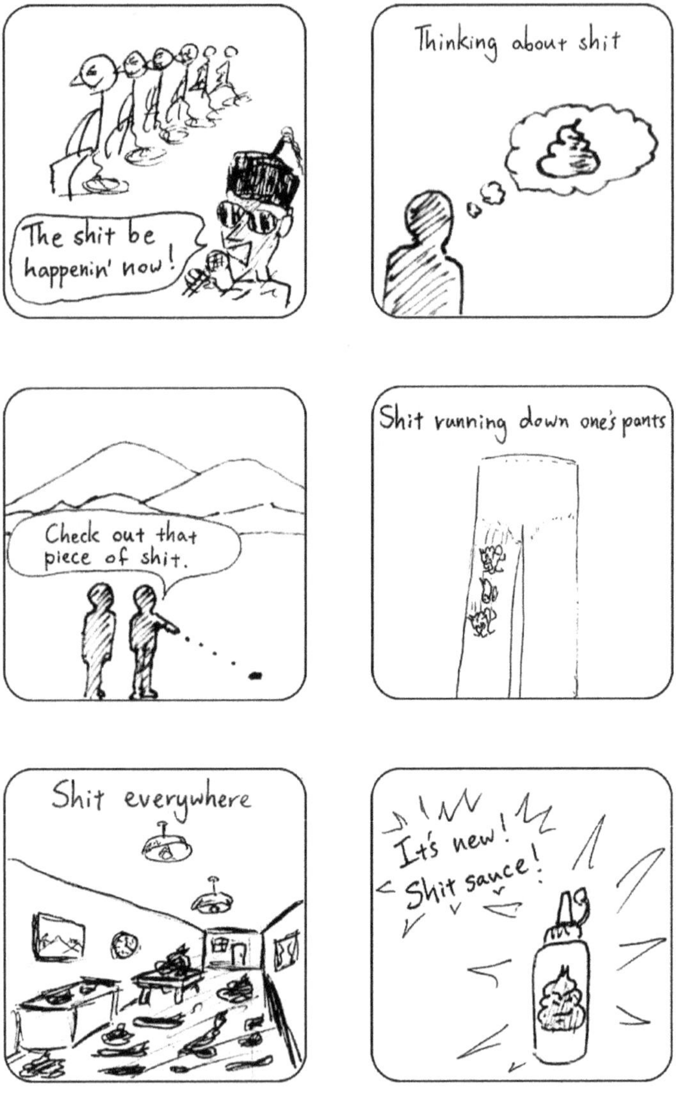
The shit be happenin' now!
Thinking about shit
Check out that piece of shit.
Shit running down one's pants
Shit everywhere
It's new!
Shit sauce!

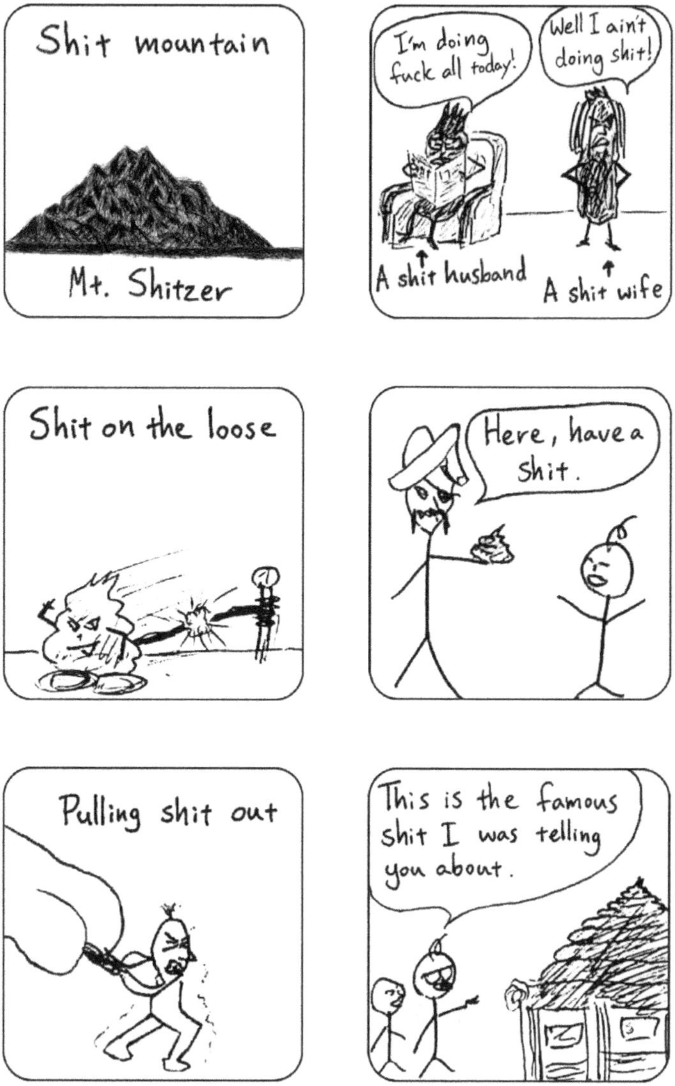
Shit mountain
Mt. Shitzer
I'm doing fuck all today!
Well I ain't doing shit!
A shit husband
A shit wife
Shit on the loose
Here, have a shit.
Pulling shit out
This is the famous shit I was telling you about.

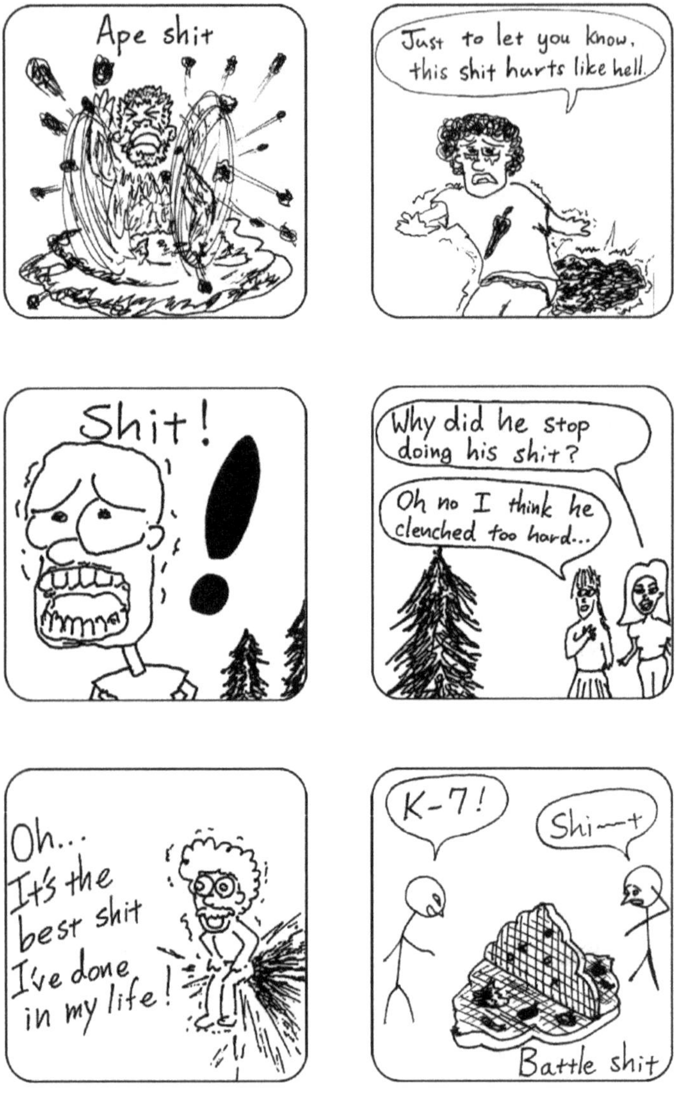
Ape shit
Just to let you know, this shit hurts like hell.
Shit!
Why did he stop doing his shit?
Oh no I think he clenched too hard...
Oh... It's the best shit I've done in my life!
K-7!
Shi—t
Battle shit

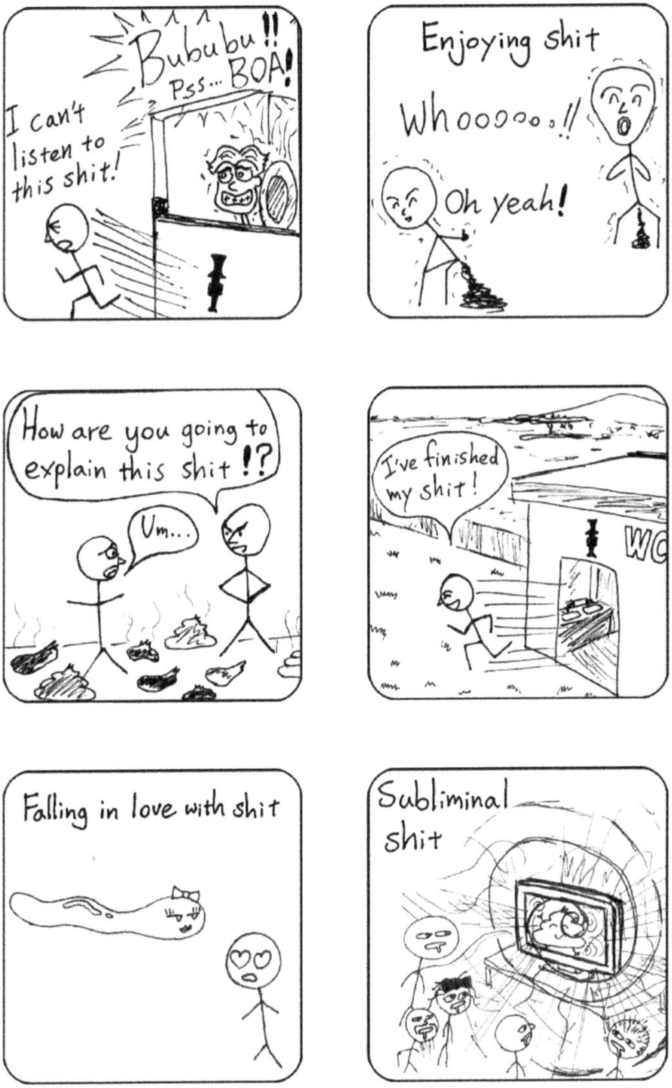
Bububu!!
Pss... BOA!
I can't listen to this shit!
Enjoying shit
Whoooooo..!!
Oh yeah!
How are you going to explain this shit!?
Um...
I've finished my shit!
WC
Falling in love with shit
Subliminal shit

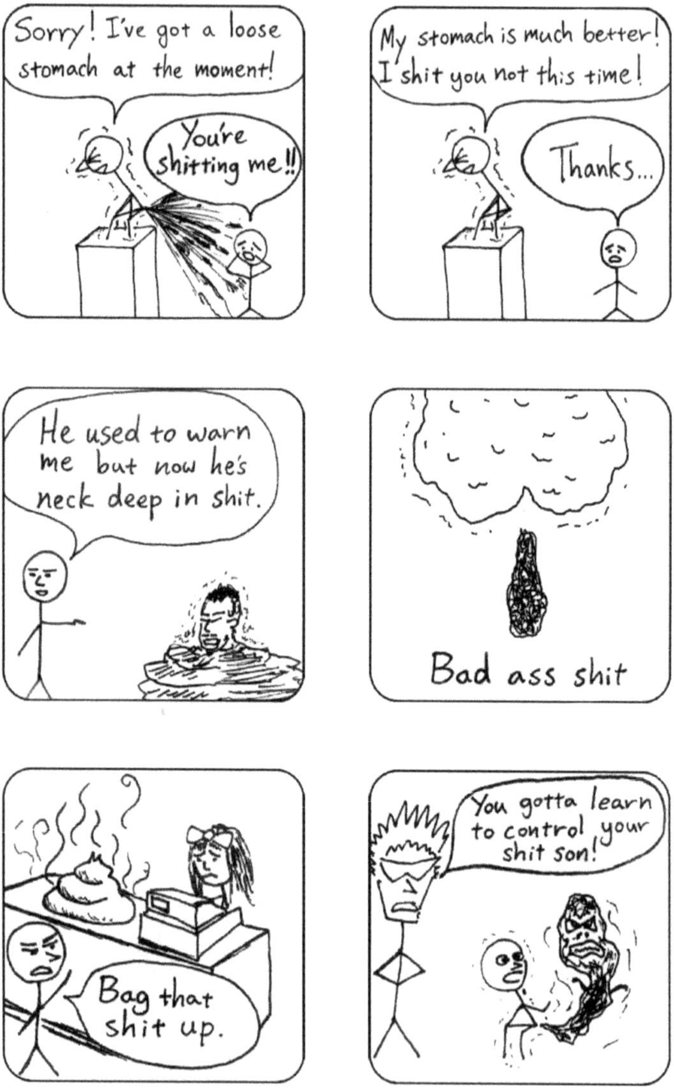
Sorry! I've got a loose stomach at the moment!
You're shitting me!!
My stomach is much better! I shit you not this time!
Thanks...
He used to warn me but now he's neck deep in shit.
Bad ass shit
Bag that shit up.
You gotta learn to control your shit son!

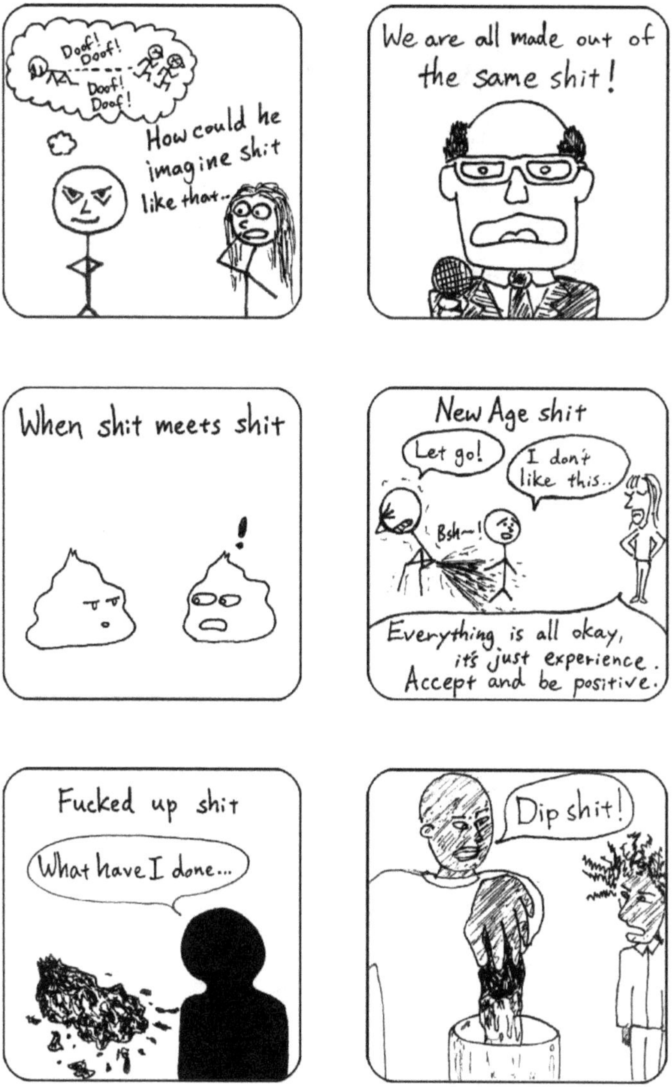
Doof! Doof!
Doof! Doof!
How could he imagine shit like that...
We are all made out of the same shit!
When shit meets shit
New Age shit
Let go!
I don't like this..
Bsh~!
Everything is all okay, it's just experience. Accept and be positive.
Fucked up shit
What have I done...
Dip shit!

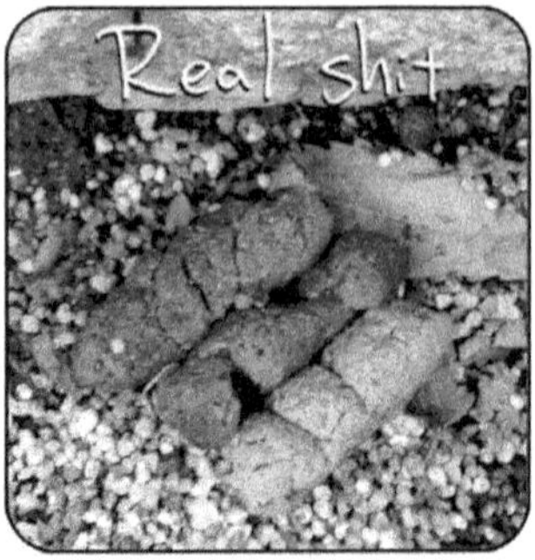
Real shit

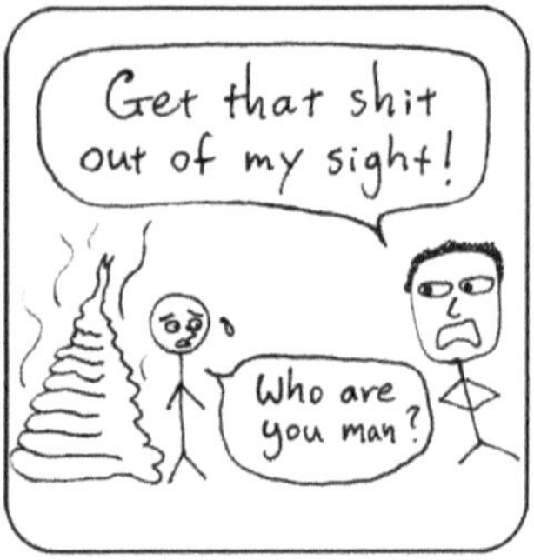
Get that shit out of my sight!
Who are you man?

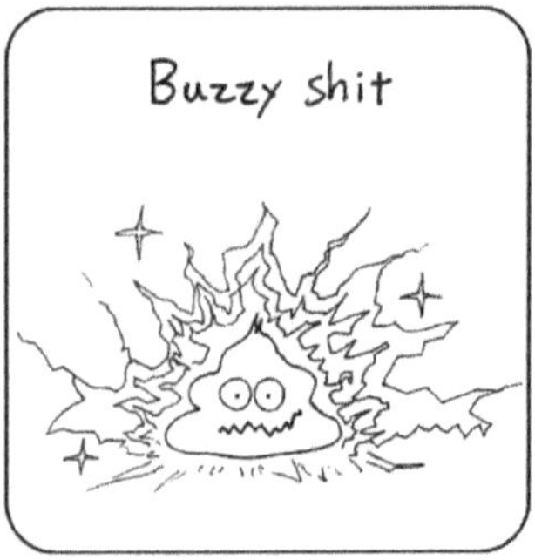
Buzzy shit

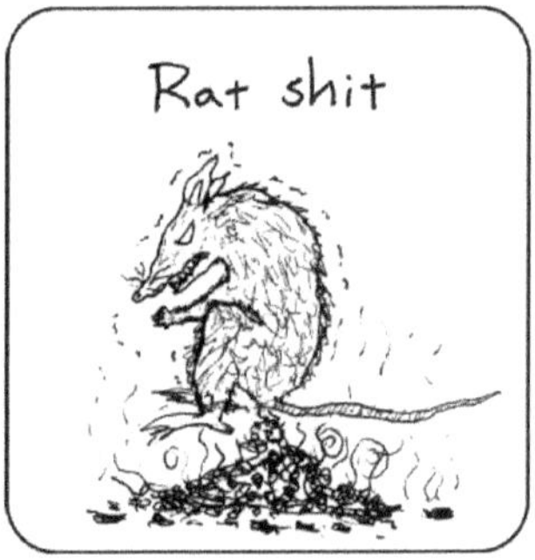
Rat shit

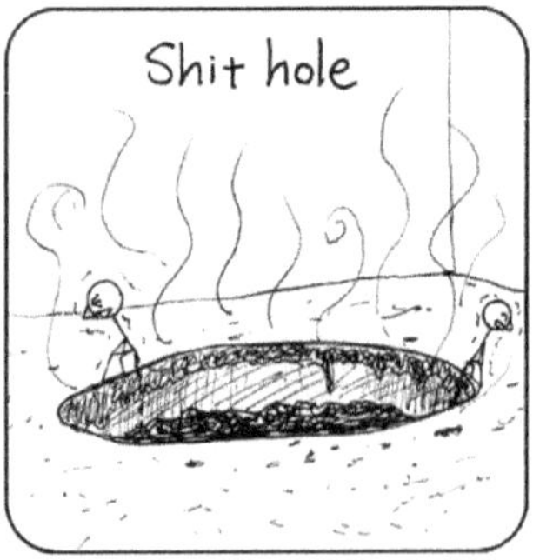
Shit hole

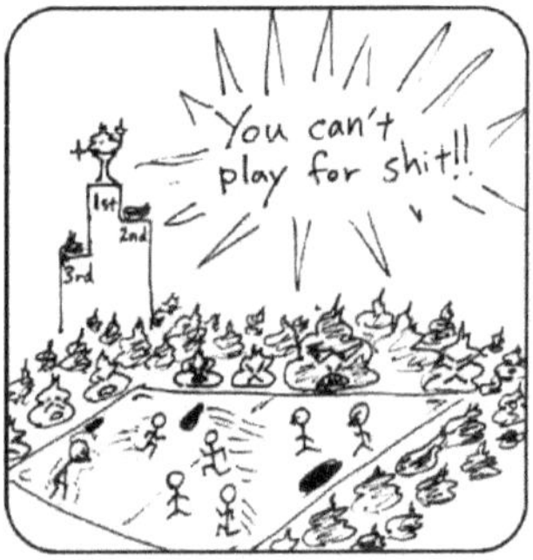
You can't play for shit!!
1st
2nd
3rd

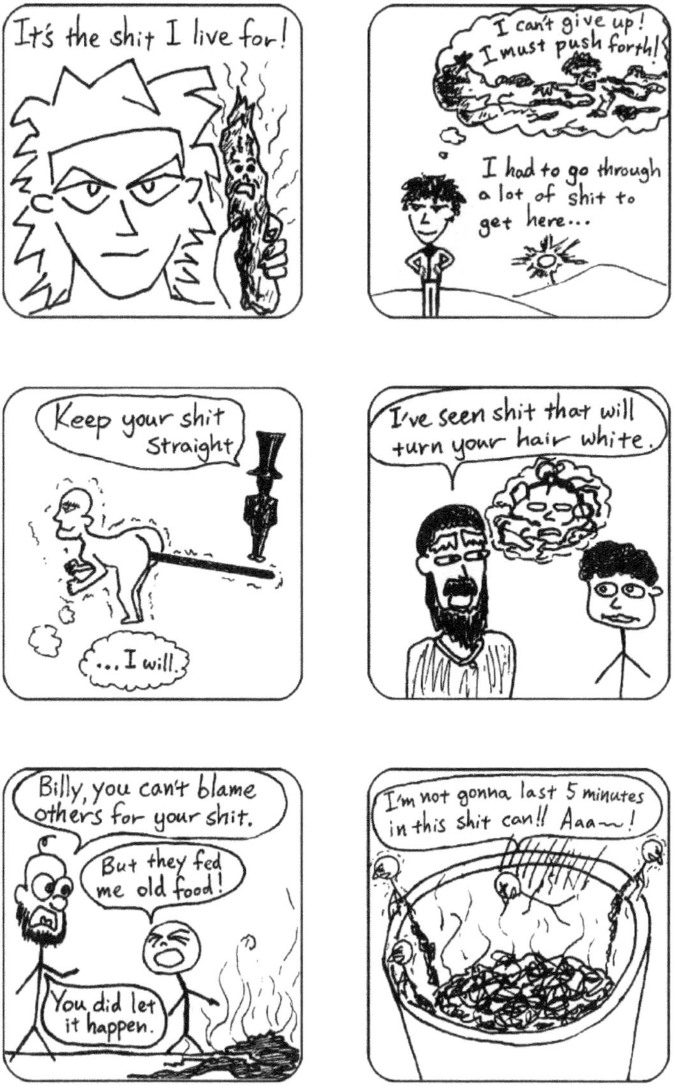
It's the shit I live for!
I can't give up! I must push forth!
I had to go through a lot of shit to get here...
Keep your shit straight.
...I will.
I've seen shit that will turn your hair white.
Billy, you can't blame others for your shit.
But they fed me old food!
You did let it happen.
I'm not gonna last 5 minutes in this shit can!! Aaa—!

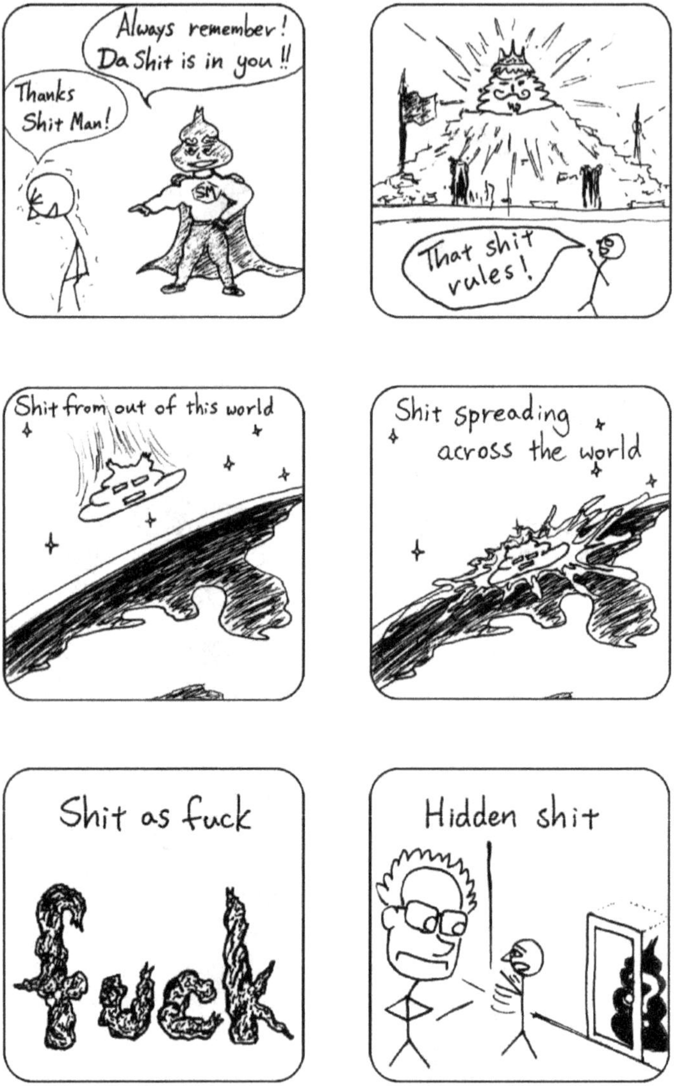
Thanks Shit Man!
Always remember! Da Shit is in you!!
SM
That shit rules!
Shit from out of this world
Shit spreading across the world
Shit as fuck
fuck
Hidden shit

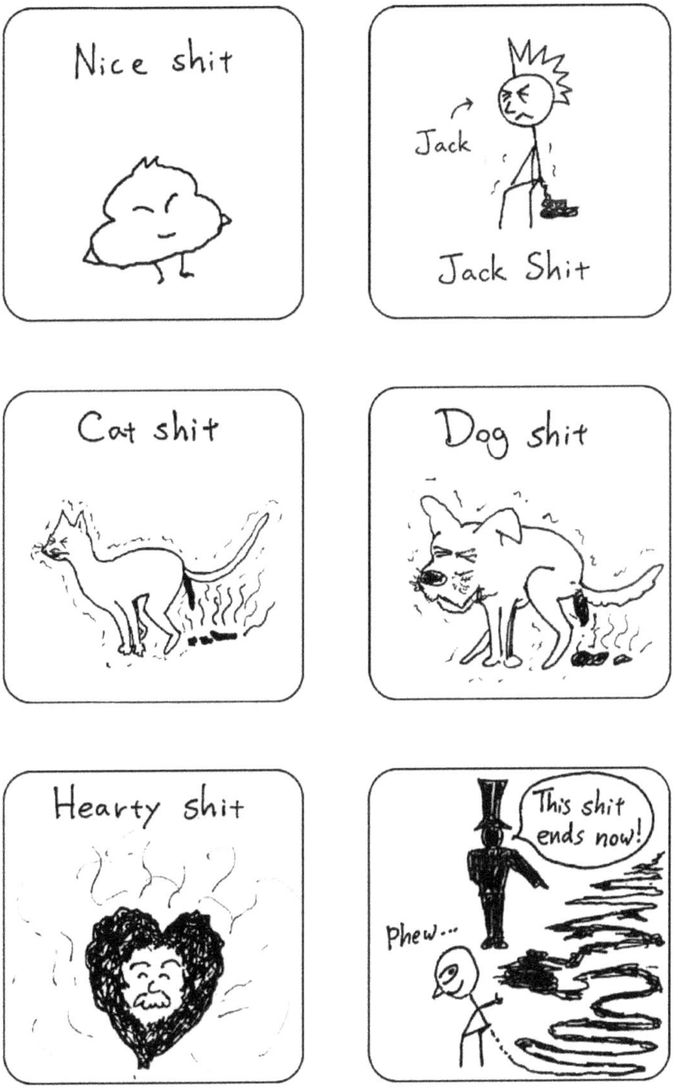
Nice shit
Jack
Jack Shit
Cat shit
Dog shit
Hearty shit
This shit ends now!
Phew...

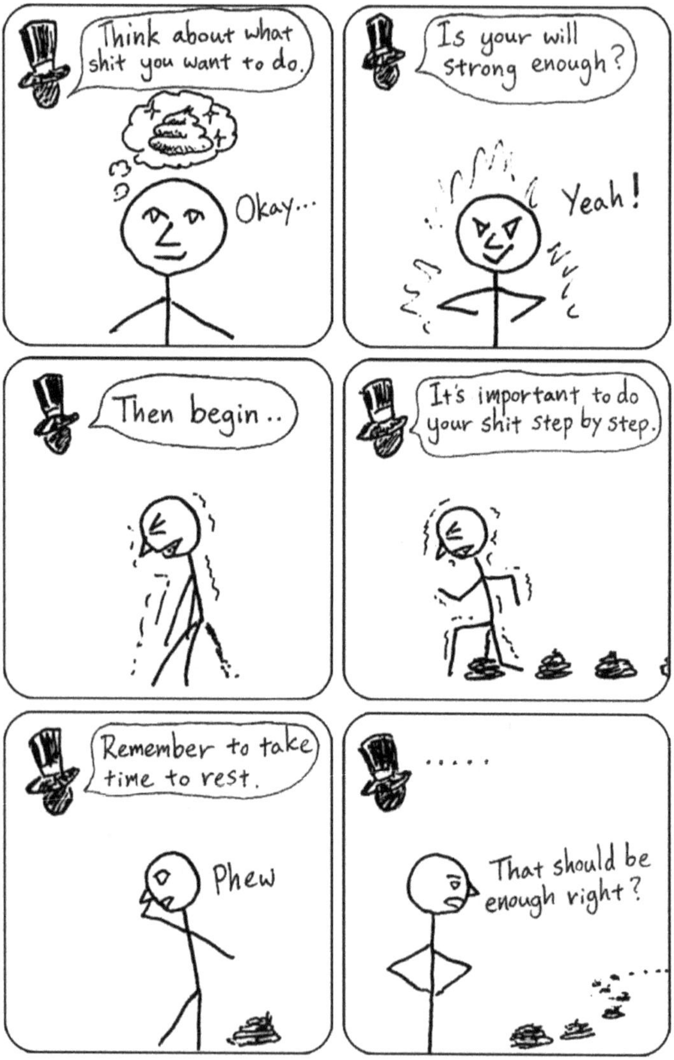
Think about what shit you want to do.
Okay...
Is your will strong enough?
Yeah!
Then begin..
It's important to do your shit step by step.
Remember to take time to rest.
Phew
.....
That should be enough right?

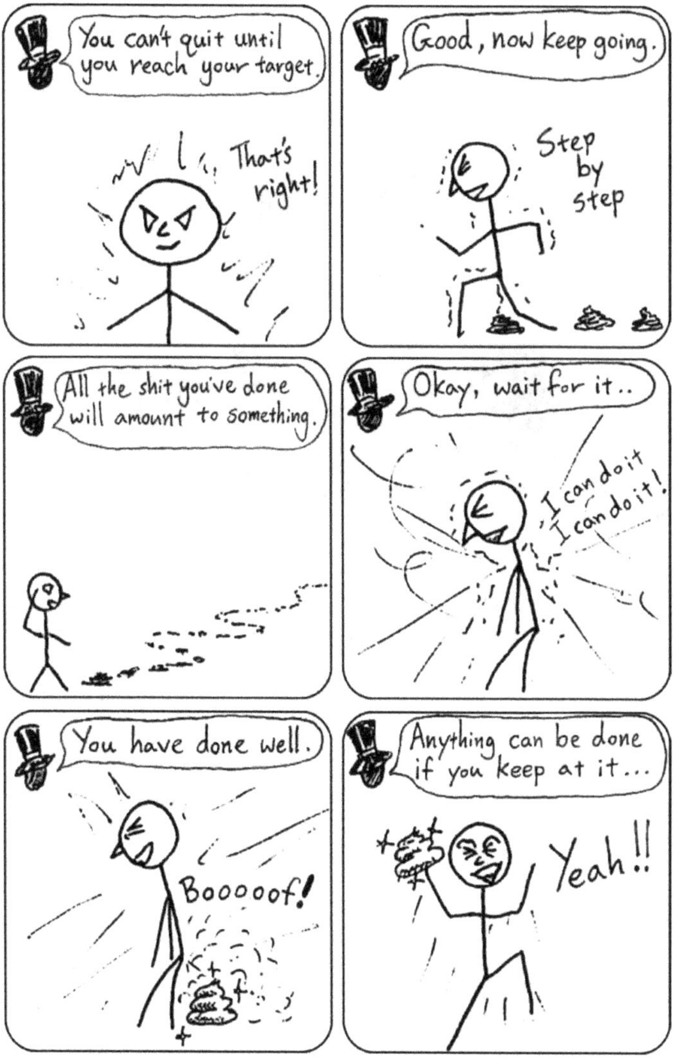
You can't quit until you reach your target.
That's right!
Good, now keep going.
Step by step
All the shit you've done will amount to something.
Okay, wait for it..
I can do it I can do it!
You have done well.
Booooof!
Anything can be done if you keep at it...
Yeah!!

DA SHIT

"Thanks for reading this book!"

Marko Poloznich

www.ingramcontent.com/pod-product-compliance
Lightning Source LLC
Chambersburg PA
CBHW060212050426
42446CB00013B/3056